W9-DID-090

CRIME SCENE PHOTOGRAPHY

Criminal Investigations Series

Steven Staggs

Copyright ©2005 Steven Staggs

[All rights reserved. No part of this publication may be reproduced, stored in a retrieval system or transmitted, in any form or by any means, whether electronic, mechanical, photocopying, recording, or otherwise, without prior written permission from the publisher.]

LawTech Custom Publishing Co., Inc.

(949)498-4815   Fax: (949)498-4858

E-mail: info@LawTechCustomPublishing.com

www.LawTechCustomPublishing.com

Comments and suggestions are welcome.

ver. 07.21.06

pp. 238

ISBN: 1-889315-27-3

Dedication

This book is dedicated to Crime Scene Investigators who strive daily to bring criminals to justice and closure to victims and their families.

Acknowledgements

I would like to thank my daughter, Sara, for assisting me with the formulation of discussion questions for this book. Sara, you are my inspiration, and I know you will do well in forensic science. Thank you, Karen, for editing my work and encouraging me during this project. Most of all, I thank God for giving me the opportunity to serve in law enforcement, the skills He has given me, and the ability to pass my experiences and skills on to others.

About the Author
Steven Staggs

For the past 20 years, Mr. Staggs has been a forensic photography instructor and has trained more than 3,500 crime scene technicians and investigators for police and sheriffs departments, district attorneys offices, and federal agencies. He is also a guest speaker for investigators' associations and provides consulting to law enforcement agencies.

The author has extensive experience in crime scene photography and identification. He has testified in superior court concerning his crime scene, evidence, and autopsy photography and has handled high profile cases including a nationally publicized serial homicide case.

Steve is the author of the "Crime Scene and Evidence Photographer's Guide," a field handbook for crime scene and evidence photography, which is in use by investigators in more than 1,000 law enforcement agencies.

He retired in 2004 after 32 years in law enforcement, but continues to teach forensic photography and crime scene investigations at universities in Southern California.

Contents at a Glance

Contents

Chapter 9   Evidence Photography In The Laboratory, 199

Chapter 1

Introduction

OVERVIEW

Crime scene photography is one of the most important aspects of documenting crime scenes and evidence. Photographs are often used as courtroom exhibits to support witnesses' testimony and to prove or disprove issues or theories before the court. Because of their value as court exhibits, the crime scene photographer's goal should be to take photographs that meet the requirements for admissibility in court.

OBJECTIVES

In this chapter you will learn about:
1. The value of crime scene and evidence photography
2. The admissibility of photographic evidence in court
3. Testifying in court
4. Becoming an expert witness

THE VALUE OF CRIME SCENE PHOTOGRAPHY

It was a fairly quiet evening in the dispatch center until all at once the 9-1-1 calls started coming in. The callers reported hearing men shouting, then screams and someone calling out for help.

The police responded to find a bleeding man with several wounds caused by some type of cutting instrument. The victim said he was attacked by two men with a large knife or hatchet. He did not know who the attackers were, he did not get a look at their faces, it was dark and the attackers wore hooded sweatshirts.

A few minutes later, and a few blocks away, a police officer stopped two men wearing hooded sweatshirts. One had a cut on his hand. After the men gave conflicting statements regarding why they were in the neighborhood, and they could not explain the cut on the hand, they were taken into custody and transported to the police station.

A crime scene investigator was called to assist in the case. The investigator went to the crime scene to photograph the area, including bloodstain on the sidewalk. Next, a machete found in the bushes a few yards away was photographed and collected as evidence. The investigator then proceeded to the emergency room to photograph the victim's injuries and collect his bloodstained clothing.

The next stop for the investigator was the police station. The investigator photographed the men in custody, one at a time. Photographs were taken to show their faces and the clothing they were wearing. The investigator observed bloodstain on their clothing and on their shoes. Several photographs were taken of the bloodstain before the suspects' shoes and clothing were collected as evidence. The crime scene investigator also photographed the cut on the one suspect's hand.

The next day, in the laboratory, the crime scene investigator photographed each item of clothing that had been collected the night before. Close-up photographs were taken to show the presence and patterns of bloodstain. The machete was photographed to show its size and the location of bloodstain on its blade and handle.

Months later, after the victim's injuries had healed, the case went to trial. Even though the victim could not identify his attackers in court, the jury found both defendants guilty of aggravated assault. When interviewed by the news media, a juror said the jury was convinced the defendants were the attackers once the photographs of bloodstain on the defendants' clothing were displayed in the courtroom, and that the jury felt the victim's injuries had been severe after viewing the injury photographs.

As we can see from this example, photography is a valuable tool for recording crime scenes and explaining evidence to others. From documenting assault scenes to recording the detail of bloodstain and injuries, photographs can communicate more about crime scenes and the appearance of evidence than the written report.

A BRIEF HISTORY OF CRIME SCENE PHOTOGRAPHY

Photography has been an effective tool in the investigation of crime scenes for more than a century. While the French police began making daguerreotypes (an early form of photograph) for identifying known criminals in 1841, the first crime scene cameras were used as early as 1865. The first crime scene cameras were large, tripod-mounted, 8" x 10" glass-plate-negative cameras.

The first handheld camera, the Speed Graphic, was introduced in 1912 and became the camera of choice for crime scene photography. Photographs were taken with ambient light or by using flash powders (explosive powders that produced a great deal of smoke) until photoflash bulbs were developed in 1930.

Specialized evidence photography began in 1902 when photographs of bullets removed from a murder victim were matched with a photograph of a test bullet from a suspect's gun. In 1905, a camera was developed for close-up photographs of fingerprints; and in 1910, the first fingerprint photograph was used in court. Ultraviolet photography was used in 1934 to photograph bloody shoe prints at a crime scene. The photograph was accepted in court to link the suspect's shoes with the crime scene.

Black and white photography was the only film used for crime scenes and evidence photography until color photographs were accepted in court in 1943.

Crime scene photography in 1867.

Crime scene photographer with camera equipment typically used in the 1960s.

Electronic flash became available in 1965 while Speed Graphic cameras were being replaced with medium format and 35 mm cameras. In the early 1970s police departments began using video cameras to document crime scenes. In the 1990s police departments began the move to digital photography for many crime scene and evidence applications.

As cameras and lighting systems improved over the last century, crime scene photographers progressed from taking one or two photographs at major crime scenes in the late 1800s to taking numerous high quality photographs, even at minor crime scenes, today.

ADMISSIBILITY OF PHOTOGRAPHS IN COURT

One of most important reasons crime scene investigators photograph crime scenes and evidence is to later use the photographs in court. These courtroom exhibits are often used to support a witness's testimony and to prove or disprove issues or theories before the court. Therefore, a goal for each photograph taken is that the photograph will be admissible in court.

Over the years, United States courts have ruled that there are three major points of qualification for a photograph to be admitted into court. All three points of qualification must be met or the photograph will be ruled inadmissible.

First, *the object pictured must be material or relevant to the point in issue*. This means the photograph must relate to testimony or a court presentation at the time it is offered as a court exhibit. Unless the content of the photograph is relevant to the point in issue, it cannot be admitted into evidence.

Second, *the content of the photograph must not appeal to the emotions or tend to prejudice the court or jury*. This means a photograph that is so terribly shocking that its use in the trial would cause the court or jury to make an unwarranted judgment cannot be admitted into evidence.

Third, *the photograph must be free from distortion and not misrepresent the scene or the object it purports to reproduce*. This means photographs admitted into evidence must be true and accurate representations of the crime scene or evidence. Distorted or misleading photographs cannot be admitted into evidence.

As you consider these three major points of qualification needed for photographs to be admitted in court, you will notice that the first two points of qualification are not the crime scene photographer's responsibility. The trial attorneys will decide whether or not to use a photograph and when they will attempt to introduce it as evidence. Then it is up to the judge to rule if the photograph is material or relevant to the point in issue. If an attorney argues that a photograph will prejudice the jury, it is up to the judge to rule if the photograph will be admitted.

The third point of qualification, *the photograph must be free from distortion and not misrepresent the scene or the object it purports to reproduce,* is an issue that relates directly to the crime scene photographer. All the photographs taken by the crime scene photographer must be true and accurate representations of the crime scene or evidence since all photographs have the potential of being used in court.

The type or style of photography used in photographing crime scenes and evidence is called technical photography. Crime scene photographers must take high quality technical photographs to ensure the photographs can be used in the investigation and ultimately in court. In the next chapter technical photography will be discussed in more detail.

Some people who read the second point of qualification of a photograph in court (the content of the photograph must not appeal to the emotions or tend to prejudice the court or jury) may wonder if crime scene photographers should avoid taking photographs that could be ruled inadmissible. The answerer is, of course, no. The crime scene photographer must photograph every scene thoroughly, showing every detail necessary to document the crime scene and evidence, including the gruesome aspects of abuse and murder.

There have been times in history when gruesome photographs were ruled inadmissible. In fact, as recently as the early 1970's, crime scene photographers used black-and-white film to photograph bloody crime scenes because color photographs were too shocking to be admitted in court. However, in recent years few photographs have been ruled inadmissible due to their shocking content. In the late 1980's, the author was the lead crime scene investigator in a spree homicide case. The suspect attacked four victims in a period of five days, beating three of them to death with a hammer. When the case went to trial, the District Attorney presented as evidence several photographs of the victims and bloody crime scenes. The defense attorneys objected to the use of the photographs on the grounds that the photographs were too shocking for the jury to arrive at a fair verdict. The judge overruled the objection stating "I believe the jury needs to understand the brutality of these crimes."

Admissibility of Digital Photographs

When digital imaging is considered for law enforcement, concern over the admissibility of digital photographic evidence in court is often raised. The fact that digital photographs are more easily altered than film-based photographs is usually cited. Some even believe digital photographs are not admissible in court. This is simply not true. Digital photographs are admissible in court. The Federal Rules of Evidence allow the use of digital images as do the rules of evidence in most states.

Also, several court decisions, including the *State of Washington vs. Eric Hayden* (1995), have accepted the use of digital photographs in court. In Hayden's homicide trial the defense specifically objected to the use of digital photographs on the grounds that some of the digital images were manipulated. The court authorized the use of digital imaging and the defendant was found guilty. In 1998, the Appellate Court upheld Hayden's conviction on appeal. Another case of note is the *State of California vs. Phillip Lee Jackson* (1995), in which a police department used digital image processing on a fingerprint in a double homicide case. When defense asked for a hearing to challenge the use of digital processing, the court ruled a hearing was unnecessary because digital processing was a readily accepted practice in forensics and that new information was not added to the image.

TESTIFYING IN COURT

All it takes for a photograph to be admitted into court (after it passes the three points of qualification previously discussed) is for someone, under oath, to say the photograph is a fair and accurate representation of what ever the photograph shows. In fact, you do not have to testify or even be present in court for your photographs to be admitted as evidence.

If you do testify in court concerning your crime scene or evidence photography, you will be testifying as either an expert witness or a non-expert witness. An expert witness is a person who has a level of knowledge, training and experience which creates an understanding of facts that are outside the abilities of the average individual. An expert witness may state opinions about the meaning of facts, even though the expert may not have observed the events. For example, a crime scene investigator who has been qualified as an expert witness in arson investigations may state opinions about the cause of a fire. Non-expert witnesses are limited to testifying about facts they observed and may not give their opinions on the meaning of those facts.

To be an expert witness, you must be qualified by the court. During the trial the District Attorney will make a motion to qualify you as an expert and ask you questions regarding the extent of your knowledge, training and experience. During the qualification process you should state something like "my knowledge of photography is limited to what I must know to perform my duties as a crime scene technician." This is because photography is a vast field and it is unlikely the average crime scene photographer will have knowledge and training to be qualified as an expert in photography. To be qualified as an expert in photography, you might be required to discuss your training in physics and chemistry, as well as answer questions on the design of lenses, composition of film emulsion, and chemistry of development. Instead of attempting to be qualified as an expert in photography, you should be qualified as an expert in crime scene identification or in crime scene photography.

SUMMARY

Today's crime scene photographers have some of the best tools and technology available for documenting crime scenes and evidence. Quality photographs taken by investigators can be used in investigations to apprehend suspects and in the court to convict them.

DISCUSSION QUESTIONS

1. When was ultraviolet photography introduced and for what purpose was it used?
2. What role does photography have in courtroom exhibits?
3. What should be the goal for each photograph taken?
4. What are the three points of qualification for a photograph to be admitted as an exhibit in court?
5. Which of the three points of qualification for admissibility does the photographer have control over? Why?
6. Who has control over the remaining points of qualification?
7. What style of photography is used for photographing crime scenes? Why?
8. Are digital photographs admissible in court?
9. Does the photographer have to testify in court in order to have a photograph entered as evidence?
10. What qualifies someone as an expert witness?

EXERCISES and ACTIVITIES

1. Research on the Internet the first reported photograph and be prepared to present the search results.
2. Start a "photo log" for the class. The first assignment is to take pictures of your residence, vehicle and a self-portrait.
3. Read the user manual for your camera and become familiar with the functions of it.

ADDITIONAL RESOURCES

Duckworth, John E., (1983) *Forensic Photography*, Charles C. Thomas, Springfield, Illinois 62717

Miller, Larry S., (1998) *Police Photography*, Fourth Edition, Anderson Publishing Co., Cincinnati, Ohio 45202

ADDITIONAL WEBSITE RESOURCES

Chapter 2

Camera And Lighting

OVERVIEW

A mentioned in the first chapter, a standard for photographs of crime scenes and evidence is that the photographs must be of sufficient quality to be admissible in a court of law. Crime scene photographers must understand how to get the correct results when using their cameras and lighting equipment for a variety of subjects and in a variety of lighting conditions.

OBJECTIVES

In this chapter you will learn about:
1. The camera
2. Technical photography
3. Flash illumination
4. Painting with light
5. Nighttime available light photography

THE CAMERA

The camera used most often in crime scene investigations is the 35mm camera. Many 35mm cameras are relatively inexpensive and produce high quality photographs. Digital cameras are now used by many agencies.

Film-Based vs. Digital

Many law enforcement and investigative agencies have moved from film-based to digital cameras. Digital photography is a viable method for documenting crime scenes and evidence. It is believed that at some point in the future the majority of agencies will use digital photography to document crimes scenes and evidence.

All of the techniques in this book can be performed with digital cameras. However, for adequate results the choice of digital camera is important. Digital cameras that have four megapixel, or greater, image sensors and manual exposure settings (in addition to any automatic or programmed exposure modes) are usually suitable for crime scene and evidence photography.

One of the most important considerations in selecting digital cameras is the quality of the image sensor. Most image sensors that are four megapixels or greater can produce photographs capable of enlargement to 16" x 20" for court exhibits. There are many other factors involved in the quality of digital photographs that also must be considered when selecting digital photography equipment, such as close-up capabilities, availability of accessories and even the printer used to print the digital photograph.

Automatic vs. Manual Photography

Most modern cameras have dependable automatic exposure systems built right in the camera. Ninety percent or more of the photographs taken at most crime scenes can be accomplished with a camera set in an automatic mode. It does become necessary, however, to know when the automatic functions of the camera will result in poor photographs so you can make adjustments or change techniques (more information about exposure adjustments and techniques are presented in the next section of this chapter).

TECHNICAL PHOTOGRAPHY

The type or style of photography used in photographing crime scenes and evidence is called "technical photography." Crime scene photographers must take high quality technical photographs to ensure the photographs can be used in the investigation and ultimately in court.

Figure 2.1 Technical Photography

Technical photographs

1. Correct exposure
2. Maximum depth of field
3. Free from distortion
4. Sharp focus

Technical photographs are photographs that show as much detail or information about the view or object pictured as possible. The best technical photographs have four characteristics. They are correctly exposed, have maximum depth of field, are free from distortion, and are in sharp focus. While frequently there are conditions that make this difficult or impossible (e.g., close-up photographs will always have shallow depth of field), crime scene and evidence photographers must strive to take photographs with these characteristics.

Correct Exposure

Technical photographs must be correctly exposed. Correct exposures are necessary for the film to capture detail in all parts of a scene, including highlight areas and shadows. Underexposed photographs lose detail in the shadows while overexposed photographs lose detail in the highlight areas.

The shutter speed and lens aperture controls exposure. Most cameras can be operated in manual and automatic modes. Automatic systems and automatic flash units produce adequate results in most normal situations. However, in some situations the automatic exposure systems may produce incorrect exposures. Some common problem lighting situations to be aware of include highly reflective scenes, bright sun-lighted scenes with deep shadows, and back lighting. In these situations you should consider metering off an 18 percent gray card, bracketing exposures, or flash fill.

Ambient light (existing light) exposures can often be metered with the camera's internal exposure meter or an external exposure meter. However, before relying on any reflected light exposure meter, you should determine if the meter will be providing an accurate reading due to the subject or background about to be photographed. Exposure meters use 18 percent reflectance in determining exposure. If you are photographing a scene that does not have 18 percent reflectance, the exposure reading can be in error. For example, when photographing a crime scene in the snow, an exposure meter will, as always, base its exposure settings on 18 percent reflectance. Since the subject matter in the photograph is almost all white, the meter will provide exposure settings that result in an underexposed photograph. Much of the detail in the photograph will be lost. A second example would be a dark area of a scene, such as a section of charred wall at an arson scene. The exposure meter will base its settings on 18 percent reflectance and would provide exposure setting that result in an overexposed photograph. Much of the detail in the charred wall will be lost.

Camera metering systems tend to underexpose highly reflective scenes, such as this crime scene located in the snow.

Metering off an 18 percent gray card will provide the correct exposure for the scene.

When using ambient light for crime scene photographs you can ensure accurate exposures by using an 18 percent gray card. Position the 18 percent gray card in front of the exposure meter, or in front of the camera lens if you are using the camera's exposure meter, to obtain the correct exposure settings. Be sure the ambient light is falling on the 18 percent gray card the same as it is falling on your scene. Use the settings indicated by the exposure meter for the photograph. If you are using a camera in an automatic exposure mode press the "automatic exposure lock" (AEL) button on the camera while pointing the lens at the gray card to lock the exposure settings for the photograph.

In many lighting situations, bracketing exposures should also be considered. Bracketing will provide a series of photographs at different exposures. Later, the best exposures from the series of photographs can be used for the investigation.

Scenes with bright sunlight produce deep shadows that can conceal evidence. This photograph was the result of the camera's automatic exposure selection. While the overall exposure is acceptable, the shadow areas conceal detail.

Bracketing can provide exposures that reveal evidence in highlight areas or shadow areas. This photograph was overexposed by two f/stops to lighten the shadow area and clearly show the evidence.

Bracketing involves making a series of exposures of the same subject at different exposures, usually at one stop or one-half stop intervals. Some cameras can be set to automatically bracket at selected exposure differences from the metered exposure.

See the camera operator's manual for information on obtaining correct exposures in different lighting situations.

Another valuable technique for insuring accurate exposures, especially for scenes with deep shadows, is flash fill. In scenes illuminated by bright sunlight there will usually be dark shadow areas. Sometimes evidence is located in the shadows. Detail in the deep shadow areas may be lost when the exposure is based on the overall brightness of the scene. With the use of flash fill, the brightness level in the shadow areas can be raised to the overall brightness of the scene.

Without flash fill, detail in shadow areas is lost.

With flash fill, detail in the shadow areas is recorded.

Many cameras with dedicated TTL (through-the-lens) flash systems can provide automatic flash fill. If you have a dedicated TTL flash system consult the equipment instruction manual for instructions on using flash fill in the camera's automatic exposure mode.

Figure 2.2 Flash Fill

1. Set the shutter speed to the camera's flash synchronization speed.

2. Use the camera's exposure meter to determine the correct f/stop for the shutter speed selected. Set that f/stop on your lens.

3. With the flash on manual, find the flash-to-subject distance for the f/stop that was selected.

4. Position the flash unit at that distance from the shadow area and take the photograph.

You can also use a camera and an electronic flash unit in manual modes for flash fill. First you must set the camera's shutter speed to the camera's flash synchronization speed (usually 1/60 or 1/125 second). Then use the camera's exposure meter to determine the correct f/stop for the shutter speed selected. Set that f/stop on your lens. With the flash on "manual", find the flash-to-subject distance for the f/stop that was selected (the flash-to-subject distance for each f/stop is usually displayed in a chart on the back of the electronic flash). Position the flash unit at that distance from the shadow area and take the photograph.

You may wish to use a flash remote cord so you can have more flexibility in choosing the proper angle to direct the electronic flash into the shadows.

Maximum Depth-of-Field

Technical photographs must have maximum depth of field. Depth of field, often called the plane of sharpness, is the area in a photograph where objects are in sharp focus. Crime scene and evidence photographs should have as much in focus as possible (a deep plane of sharpness). This is because out-of-focus areas of a photograph can become issues in court. An opposing attorney could suggest that you purposely caused an area to be out of focus in a photograph to obscure some additional evidence that could have been clearly visible if properly photographed.

There are three factors that affect depth of field. They are the focal length of the lens on the camera, the camera-to-subject distance, and the lens aperture (f/stop) selected.

In crime scene and evidence photography you usually do not have much control over the first two factors that affect depth of field. While long focal length lenses (e.g., 135mm) produce shallow planes of sharpness and short focal length lenses (e.g., 28mm) produce deep planes of sharpness, you will usually be using a 50mm lens (on a 35mm camera) because it provides the best visual perspective (lens selection and perspective will be discussed in more detail later). And while short camera-to-subject distances produce shallower planes of focus than longer camera-to-subject distances, the distance between the camera and your subject will depend on what needs to be shown in the photograph. For example, close-up photographs require positioning the camera close to the subject resulting in shallow planes of sharpness.

In crime scene and evidence photography, you usually control depth of field by lens aperture (f/stop) selection. Smaller lens openings (e.g., f/22) will give you deeper planes of focus while larger lens openings (e.g., f/1.8) will give you shallower planes of focus.

Shallow plane of focus — f/1.8 was used for this photograph, which produced poor depth-of-field.

Deep plane of focus — f/22 was used for this photograph, which produced greater depth-of-field.

It is often helpful to be able to determine the area that will be in focus before you take a photograph. For example, at a homicide scene you may want to take a photograph showing the relationship between a gun on the floor and the victim's body. You have determined that the body is seven feet from the camera and the gun is 30 feet from the camera. How can you be sure that both the gun and the body will be in sharp focus? Fortunately, there are three methods to determine the depth of field before you take the photograph.

The first method to determine depth of field is by using the "depth-of-field preview lever" or button on most 35mm cameras. Pressing the depth of field preview lever allows you to manually "stop down" the lens aperture. As you look in the camera's viewfinder with the lens stopped down you will be able to see the area that will be in focus.

A second method to determine depth of field is to use the depth of field chart that is located in the owner's guide that came with your lens. The chart will show at what distances sharpness begins and ends for different f/stops and focused distances.

■ **Depth of Field**   (ft)

Focused distance	Depth of field							Reproduction ratio
	f/2.8	f/4	f/5.6	f/8	f/11	f/16	f/22	
0.85	10-1/16" — 10-5/16"	10" — 10-5/16"	9-15/16" — 10-3/8"	9-7/8" — 10-1/2"	9-3/4" — 10-5/8"	9-9/16" — 10-7/8"	9-3/8" — 11-3/16"	1/5.96
1	11-13/16" — 1'3/16"	11-11/16" — 1'1/4"	11-5/8" — 1'3/8"	11-7/16" — 1'9/16"	11-5/16" — 1'3/4"	11" — 1'11-3/16"	10-11/16" — 1'1-3/4"	1/7.6
1.5	1'5-7/16" — 1'6-9/16"	1'5-3/16" — 1'6-13/16"	1'4-7/8" — 1'7-1/4"	1'4-1/2" — 1'7-13/16"	1'4" — 1'8-5/8"	1'3-1/4" — 1'10-1/4"	1'2-1/2" — 2'9/16"	1/13
2	1'10-7/8" — 2'1-3/16"	1'10-7/16" — 2'1-13/16"	1'9-7/8" — 2'2-5/8"	1'9-1/16" — 2'4"	1'8-3/16" — 2'5-15/16"	1'6-7/8" — 2'9-15/16"	1'5-9/16" — 3'4-11/16"	1/18.3
3	2'9-1/4" — 3'3-1/4"	2'8-3/16" — 3'4-7/8"	2'6-7/8" — 3'7-5/16"	2'5-3/16" — 3'11-9/16"	2'3-5/16" — 4'6-3/8"	2'3/4" — 5'11-15/16"	1'10-5/16" — 10'5/16"	1/29
5	4'4-1/8" — 5'10-7/8"	4'1-3/8" — 6'4-15/16"	3'10-1/8" — 7'2-15/16"	3'6-1/16" — 9'7/16"	3'2" — 13'2-1/16"	2'8-13/16" — 60'8-11/16"	2'4-5/16" — ∞	1/50.3
∞	29' — ∞	20'4" — ∞	14'7" — ∞	10'4" — ∞	7'7" — ∞	5'3" — ∞	3'11" — ∞	1/∞

Depth-of-field chart located in the owner's guide for a lens.

The third method to determine depth-of-field is to check the depth of field scale engraved on most lenses (see the following illustrations).

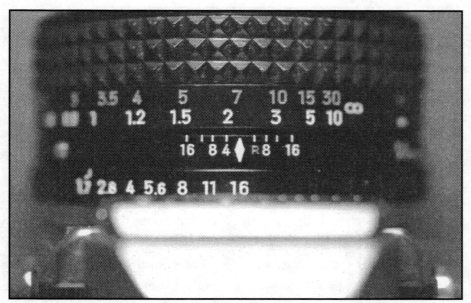

Using the depth of field scale engraved on most lenses — in this example the focus is set for a 7-foot distance. The depth-of-field scale indicates that if f/16 were in use, objects from 5 feet to 12 feet would be in focus (a relatively deep plane of focus). If f/8 were in use, objects from 6 feet to 9 feet would be in sharp focus (a shallower plane of focus).

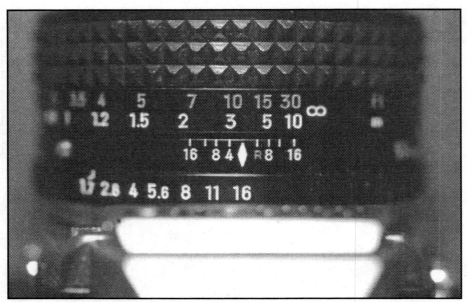

Using our example of a homicide scene and using a setting of f/16, if the body is seven feet and the gun 30 feet from the camera, we can focus at 11 feet and the depth of field scale shows that the plane of sharpness begins at seven feet and ends at 30 feet. Both the body and the gun will be in focus.

Free From Distortion

Technical photographs must be as free from distortion as possible and must have good perspective. The most common cause of distortion in photographs is improper lens selection. The lens that will provide the least distortion, and will provide photographs that look similar to what you see at the scene, is the "normal focal length lens." You should use a normal focal length lens whenever possible (a 50mm lens is considered the normal lens for a 35mm camera). Long focal length lenses give a telephoto effect, and short focal length lenses produce wide-angle distortion. Distances in photographs taken with long and short focal lenses will be deceiving; the viewer will think distances are shorter or longer than they actually were at the scene. This could create discrepancies in court when a witness testifies to a distance that appears in error when compared with a wide-angle photograph on display.

These three photographs were taken from the same location. The first photograph was taken with a 50mm lens. It provides a view that is similar to what the photographer saw at the scene.

Using a 100mm lens gives a telephoto effect causing distances to look shorter.

A 28mm lens causes distances to look longer.

Technical photographs must also have good perspective. To ensure you have good perspective you should hold the camera level and at eye level (between 4 1/2 and 6 feet above the ground) whenever possible. This provides views in photographs that are easier for others to understand. Of course there are many times that you cannot hold the camera level or at eye level. For example, you will point the camera straight down to photograph a footwear impression or position the camera near the ground to photograph evidence under a parked vehicle—but hold the camera level and at eye level when you are able.

Sharp Focus

Technical photographs must be in sharp focus. To ensure your photographs are in sharp focus, keep the camera steady during the exposure. You should mount the camera on a tripod if the shutter speed is less than 1/60-second and focus carefully. Also, maximizing depth of field will result in sharpness in a larger area of the photograph.

FLASH ILLUMINATION

Types of Flash Illumination

Manual Flash

When you use a manual flash set the lens f/stop for the flash-to-subject distance (the f/stop for each distance is usually displayed in a chart on the back of the electronic flash).

Automatic Flash

Automatic flash units use distance ranges. Each range has a minimum and maximum distance. An f/stop is assigned to each range. Changing to a new range requires a change in f/stop. When in automatic flash, make sure the camera shutter speed dial is set to the flash synchronization speed. When photographing a high key scene (light or reflective background), bracket exposures by opening up one or two f/stops.

Dedicated Flash

The basic dedicated flash unit sets the correct flash synchronization speed when the flash is in operation. It uses an automatic sensor and distance ranges. You must set the appropriate f/stop for the distance range. More advanced dedicated flash units may set both the correct flash synchronization speed and f/stop for the automatic range selected.

Dedicated TTL Flash

The dedicated TTL (through-the-lens) flash uses a sensor inside the camera to control the duration of the flash. Use smaller lens apertures for short distances and larger lens apertures for long distances. A "confidence light" or a "warning light" will indicate whether a useable f/stop was selected. If the equipment indicates there was not enough light, select a larger lens aperture and re-photograph. Dedicated TTL flash units can usually be used in manual and automatic modes, as well as TTL.

Problems With Electronic Flash Photography

Distances

Light produced by an electronic flash falls off quickly. This effect is the inverse square law of light (if the distance between the flash and subject is doubled, the illumination will drop to one quarter of the original) and results in bright foregrounds and dark backgrounds. This can be a significant problem with flash photographs outdoors at night. It may be necessary to use an automatic flash distance range that is twice the actual flash-to-subject distance or use manual flash settings (open up two f/stops). Other solutions include using a different lighting technique such as multiple flash, painting with light, or available light (utilizing existing light without electronic flash).

Reflective Surfaces

Automatic flash units can shut off too soon due to reflected light from surfaces such as tile, white walls, or chrome. To avoid an underexposed photograph you may bracket to larger lens openings, diffuse the flash, angle the flash, or use manual flash.

Bounce Flash

You can use bounce lighting for less contrast, softer lighting, reducing the intensity of the light, or to increase the angle of flash coverage. Bounce lighting is accomplished by angling the flash to reflect the flash off a white or light-colored surface, usually a ceiling. With manual flash add the distance up and down for the flash-to-subject distance, and then add in the absorbance loss (one to three f/stops). For bounce lighting utilizing an automatic flash with the flash sensor facing the subject, use a range for two or more times the actual flash-to-subject distance.

Multiple Flashes

To illuminate large areas you can get good results by using several flash units positioned around the scene. The flash units can be triggered simultaneously by connecting them with sync cords or using photocell devices that remotely trigger the flash units when the camera-mounted flash fires. To balance the intensity of each of the flash units, distance the flash units from the subject to provide the same f/stop value for each flash.

PAINTING WITH LIGHT

Painting with light is especially useful for lighting large crime scenes at night when a single flash will not provide adequate lighting coverage. Painting with light is also used at night traffic collision scenes to provide lighting for large areas.

A single electronic flash does not provide adequate coverage.

With painting with light the area of coverage is increased.

Painting with light is accomplished by opening the camera's shutter for an extended period of time while a light source is moved around until the entire scene is properly illuminated. The light source can be a flashlight or a spotlight, but the most effective light source is usually an electronic flash unit with a "test fire" button.

Figure 2.3 Painting With Light

Painting with Light

1. Mount the camera on a sturdy tripod.

2. Screw a locking cable release into the camera shutter release.

3. With the camera in the manual mode, set the shutter speed dial to B (bulb).

4. Determine the f/stop for the lens based on the flash-to-subject distance. Set that f/stop on the lens.

5. Focus carefully.

6. Depress the cable release and lock it to hold the shutter open.

7. Fire the electronic flash, by pressing the "test fire" button, to light areas of the scene.

8. Unlock the cable release and allow the shutter to close.

Painting with light is done with both the camera and electronic flash in their manual modes. First you mount the camera on a sturdy tripod. Attach a locking cable release to the camera (some cameras require an electronic cable release or have an extended time function built in to the camera—see your camera's instruction manual for further information). Set the shutter speed to the "B" (bulb) setting. Determine the f/stop needed for the exposure based on the flash-to-subject distance (not the camera-to-subject distance) you will be using. For example, if you plan to position the flash about 20 feet away from each area you intend to illuminate, select the f/stop for that distance (the f/stop for each distance is usually displayed in a chart on the back of the electronic flash). Focus carefully. Depress the cable release and lock it to hold the shutter open. Fire the electronic flash, by pressing the "test fire" button, to light areas of the scene. The number of flashes and angle of the flashes will depend on the size and character of the scene. Do not point the flash directly at the camera and keep yourself out of the view of the camera. When you finish lighting the scene, unlock the cable release allowing the shutter to close.

If there will be vehicle traffic through the scene during the painting with light exposure, the streaking of headlights and taillights will record in the photograph. In such situations you may wish to cover the camera lens between flashes to block out the lights from vehicle traffic.

AVAILABLE LIGHT PHOTOGRAPHY

Available light photography is especially useful for large crime scenes at night when a single flash will not provide adequate coverage. Lighting for the photograph may be from street lamps, parking lot lamps, or even moonlight. Available light from street lamps is frequently used at night traffic collision scenes to provide lighting for large areas.

Single electronic flash, does not provide adequate coverage.

Using an available light exposure, area of coverage is increased.

You may be able to get an adequate exposure meter reading to operate your camera in manual settings. Automatic cameras may also operate in low-light conditions. Many supplementary exposure meters provide accurate readings in very low-light conditions.

When obtaining an exposure meter reading do not point the exposure meter directly at lights in your scene, or the photograph you take will be underexposed. Since lighting is usually contrasty at night (light sources are many times brighter than shadow areas), determine which area of the scene is most important and aim the exposure meter in that area.

Use a tripod and cable release to avoid camera movement during the exposure. Bracketing exposures will help to ensure a good photograph.

Supplementary Exposure Meter

Using the available light for a nighttime exposure, the area of coverage is normally greater than lighting from a single electronic flash.

SUMMARY

As the saying goes, practice makes perfect. In photography practice is essential not only in learning how to operate your camera equipment, but is essential in reaching and maintaining the skill levels necessary to become a crime scene photographer. Reading instructions and looking at example photographs is usually not enough. You must try the techniques and keep practicing them because practice does make perfect.

DISCUSSION QUESTIONS

1. What type of digital camera is usually suitable for crime scene and evidence photography?
2. Describe the four characteristics that technical photographs should have.
3. How is exposure controlled?
4. What is bracketing?
5. What three factors do you need to consider that affect the depth of field?
6. List the types of flash illumination.
7. List the problems with electronic flash photography and their results.
8. Describe how painting with light is accomplished.
9. What must you avoid when painting with light?
10. When using available light at night, where should you point the exposure meter so as not to underexpose your photographs?

EXERCISES and ACTIVITIES

1. Take **automatic pictures** of the following subjects:
   - A large object in the sun, from about 25' away
   - A large object in the shade, from about 25' away
   - A person standing under a shade tree, with the background and foreground in the sun, from about 25' away
   - A vehicle moving at least 40 M.P.H. during the day (Don't stand in the street)
   - A vehicle moving at least 40 M.P.H. at night (Don't stand in the street)
   - A room inside a building, without flash
   - The same room, with flash
   - A vehicle, in a parking lot, at night, using flash, about 40' away

- The same vehicle, at night, using flash, about 10' away

2. Take **manual pictures** of the following subjects:

- A large object in the sun, from about 25' away

- A large object in the shade, from about 25' away

- A person standing under a shade tree, with the background and foreground in the sun, from about 25' away

- A vehicle moving at least 40 M.P.H. during the day (Don't stand in the street)

- A vehicle moving at least 40 M.P.H. at night (Don't stand in the street)

- A room inside a building, without flash

- The same room, with flash

- With using flash, photograph an object 5' from the camera, inside a building, using the f/stop that will allow the most light to enter the camera

- Without using flash, photograph an object 5' from the camera, inside a building, using the f-stop that will allow the least light to enter the camera

- A vehicle, in a parking lot, at night, using flash, about 40' away

- The same vehicle, at night, using flash, about 10' away

3. Take pictures to correlate how f-stop and shutter speed relate to depth of field.

ADDITIONAL RESOURCES

Duckworth, John E., (1983) *Forensic Photography*, Charles C. Thomas, Springfield, Illinois 62717

London, Barbara, Upton, John, (2001) *Photography*, 7th Edition, Prentice Hall, Upper Saddle River, New Jersey 07458

McDonald, James A., (1992) *Close-up and Macro Photography for Evidence Technicians*, Second Edition, Phototext Books, Palatine, Illinois 60067

Miller, Larry S., (1998) *Police Photography*, Fourth Edition, Anderson Publishing Co., Cincinnati, Ohio 45202

Staggs, Steven, (2005) *Crime Scene and Evidence Photographer's Guide*, Second Edition, Staggs Publishing, Wildomar, California 92595

Chapter 3

Crime Scene Fundamentals

OVERVIEW

During the processing of a crime scene, several tasks and procedures must be accomplished by investigators. Documentation of the scene and its evidence with photography is only one part of the investigation of a crime scene. Photography must be employed at the correct times, and with the correct methods, during the processing of the scene.

OBJECTIVES

At the end of this chapter, you will understand the role of photography in the processing of crime scenes including:

1. The six steps in processing a crime scene
2. Documentation of the scene and its evidence with photography
3. The role of the Crime Scene Photographer
4. The use of a Photo Log
5. The tools of the trade

CRIME SCENE FUNDAMENTALS

Since virtually all crime scenes have physical evidence, the documentation of a crime scene has the potential to play a critical role in the investigation and resolution of a suspected criminal act. Crime scene investigators must approach each crime scene as if it will be their only opportunity to recover and preserve important physical evidence.

All crime scenes are unique. While most agencies have policies or guidelines for the processing of crime scenes, the judgment of investigators at the scene will ultimately determine how the scene is processed.

Scenes should be processed in a methodical manner. Generally, crime scenes are processed in the following steps:

Step 1: Crime Scene is Secured

The first step in documenting a crime scene is the securing of the scene. The scene must be preserved with minimal disturbance of the evidence. The first responder is the one most likely to assume the responsibility of securing the scene. Once the first responder has taken necessary actions to save lives and arrest suspects he must secure the crime scene to prevent destruction or alteration of evidence.

The boundaries of the crime scene must be established to prevent contamination of the scene and destruction of evidence. The area is controlled with the use of crime scene tape and the use of one entrance/exit for the scene. Boundaries should normally be made larger than first thought. Later the area can be reduced in size.

Step 2: Documentation of the Scene Begins with Field Notes

Every observation and activity at the crime scene must be documented. It is important that this documentation be done as each observation and activity occurs in order to accurately preserve information.

Documentation begins with notes and logs. Every detail is recorded. Notes are valuable in documenting things that will not appear in photographs or sketches, such as actions taken by investigators, statements made by witnesses, odors noticed, etc. Many investigators use a small tape or digital voice recorder, instead of a notebook, to record notes and observations.

A crime scene log is usually used at major crime scenes. A crime scene log is a form used to document, chronologically, the actions taken by investigators, names of those who enter and exit the scene, etc.

Step 3: Crime Scene Assessment

Investigators assess the scene to determine the level of investigation to be conducted.

Once preliminary notes have been taken, and/or a crime scene log has been started, the investigators at the scene must assess the scene to determine the level of investigation that should be conducted. This may include a walk-through conducted by the lead investigator. The assessment will include determination of what types of documentation are necessary, including notes, photography, video, measurements and sketches or diagrams. A plan is made for documenting the scene, identifying evidence and the collection of evidence.

Step 4: Documentation of the Scene Continues with Photography

Once the crime scene has been secured, preliminary notes have been taken and the scene has been assessed, photography should begin. Photography is begun early in the investigation since, when properly applied, it is a nondestructive technique. A complete set of overview photographs should be taken as soon as possible. The overview photographs should be followed with photographs of each item of evidence before it is collected.

> **Figure 3.1   The Three Step Approach**
>
> ### The Three Step Approach
>
> When photographically documenting a crime scene, it is usually best to use a three step approach:
>
> 1. Show the overall scene with *overview photographs*.
> 2. Show the location of evidence with *mid-range photographs*.
> 3. Show the details of evidence with *close-up photographs*.
>
> Using this three step approach, working from the outside of the scene in to the smallest items of evidence, will normally provide a complete photographic documentation of the crime scene and its related evidence.

The purpose of overview photographs is to enable others to visualize the scene as you, the photographer, first saw it. Plan your photographs with this in mind. Take at least one complete set of photographs before the scene is altered or disturbed. If something was moved before you arrived, do not try to reconstruct the scene before the photography. The photographs should show the scene as you found it.

Do not let investigators or crime scene equipment appear in the photographs. Be careful not to disturb or destroy any evidence while taking the photographs. This can be a difficult matter since some evidence can be difficult to see, such as dusty footwear impressions on a floor.

Outside the Scene

In cases involving crime scenes located within buildings, begin the overview photographs with the exterior of the building. In some cases you may need to photograph a large portion of the surrounding area, such as vehicles parked on streets or in parking lots, alleys, or escape routes. One of the exterior overview photographs should include an identifying landmark such as a street sign or address plaque. The series of exterior photographs should normally include all doors, windows, and other means of entrance or exit to and from the building. Aerial photographs of the scene and the surrounding area can be useful in some types of cases.

Aerial Photographs

Aerial Photograph

When taking photographs from aircraft, either fixed-wing or helicopter, use a zoom lens in order to compose your photograph without having to direct the pilot to make slight changes in altitude. Photograph through an open window or door and use exposures with relatively fast shutter speeds to avoid camera movement.

Inside the Scene

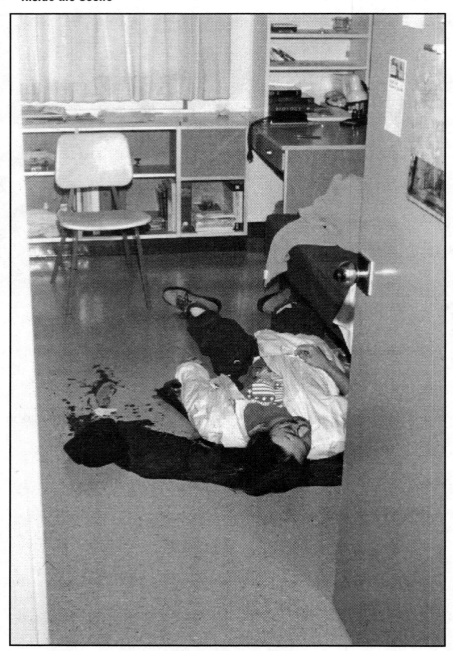

View of the entrance into the scene of a gunshot suicide

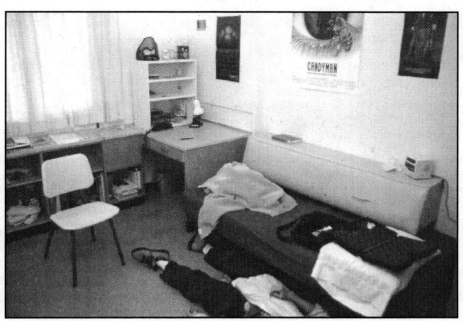

Overview photograph 1 - taken from the first corner of the room (corner nearest the entry door).

Overview photograph 2 - moving clockwise, taken from second corner of room.

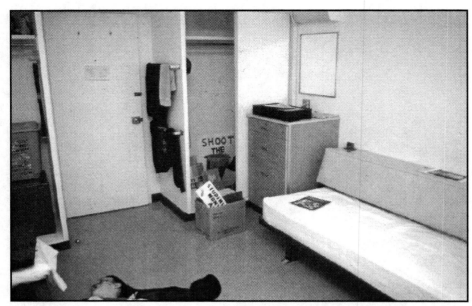

Overview photograph 3 - moving clockwise, taken from the third corner of room.

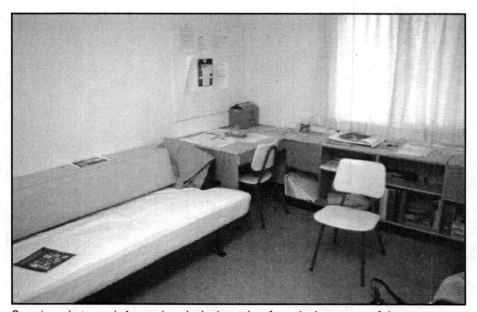

Overview photograph 4 - moving clockwise, taken from the last corner of the room.

Plan your interior overview photographs to show how things would appear to anyone walking through the scene. For each room or area, begin with a view of the entrance. Photograph the room or area as it appears when you first step inside. Take overview photographs from each corner of the room to show the layout of the room. A wide-angle lens is usually used for interior overview photographs. In large rooms you may need to take additional photographs from other locations for complete coverage.

These overview photographs, along with mid-range photographs, should also show the positions of any potential items of evidence. If the overview photographs do not show the location of a specific item of evidence, take a mid-range photograph or an additional overview photograph from another angle to show the location of the evidence. Continue with photographs of other rooms connected with the crime scene. If the crime scene is an apartment, hotel, or office, you may also want to take photographs of hallways, stairwells and similar areas.

Step 5: The Crime Scene Diagram

A crime scene diagram is started. The general area is sketched and some crime scene dimensions are recorded. Additional details, including the locations of each item of evidence, will be added to the diagram, as evidence is located during step six of the crime scene processing.

Diagrams are important because they "fill in the gaps" in the documentation of crime scenes by documenting aspects of the scene that are difficult or impossible to document with notes and photographs. Photographs show selected views while diagrams can be drawn to show a "bird's-eye view" of the entire scene. Distances are frequently misleading in photographs while diagrams are usually drawn to scale and include specific measurements. Furthermore, diagrams can be drawn to show the location of small items, making them as obvious as larger items of evidence, when their locations may be difficult to see in photographs.

Step 6: Locate, Document, and Collect Evidence

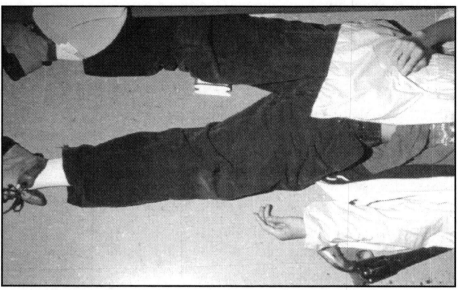

Mid-range photograph, taken to establish the location of evidence in the crime scene.

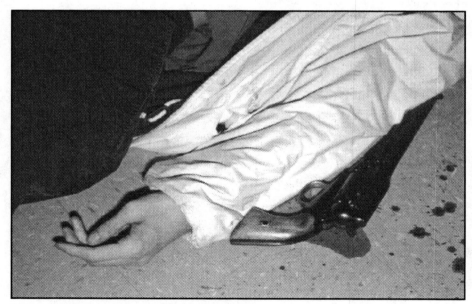

Close-up photograph, shows the details of evidence.

As each item of evidence is located, it should be documented by adding it to the notes, photographing it, and adding it to the diagram. When photographing evidence at the scene you must first show where in the scene the evidence is located. This is usually done with a mid-range photograph to establish the location of evidence and the relationship of evidence and items in the crime scene. The mid-range photograph is followed with a close-up photograph to show the details of evidence at the crime scene.

Additional Considerations

While photographing the crime scene the photographer must be aware of the theories under consideration by investigators. Many times theories can be tested through photography. One example is the view of suspects, witnesses, or victims during the incident. The photographer can place the camera at a subject's viewing position and, using a 35mm lens, demonstrate what the subject could have seen.

THE ROLE OF THE CRIME SCENE PHOTOGRAPHER

The crime scene photographer is a member of the crime scene investigation team. In some large agencies the crime scene photographer will only be responsible for the photographing of scenes and their related evidence as well as specialized photography away from the scene (e.g., laboratory and autopsy photography). In small to medium-sized agencies the crime scene photographer may be responsible for other duties at a crime scene including diagramming and evidence collection.

The crime scene photographer has a crucial role in the documenting of crime scenes and evidence. The photographs the crime scene photographer takes will be the only remaining views of a scene or evidence that can be studied days, weeks and even years after the suspected criminal act. Crime scene photographers must use their training and experience in both photography and forensics to complete a series of photographs that can be used by investigators, attorneys, and ultimately, in a court of law to clearly demonstrate what the scene and evidence looked like shortly after the crime occurred. Even if an investigator points out to the crime scene photographer what items need to be photographed, the crime scene photographer must make most of the decisions on what angles of view are needed and which techniques to use to accurately photograph the scene.

Photo Log

Notes should be taken to identify what photographs were taken and/or what each photograph was intended to show or accomplish. This record will assist the photographer in remembering what he/she was trying to demonstrate with each photograph. It will also assist others who view the photographs at a later time in understanding the photographs. For example, photographs of two similar bedrooms at a scene are differentiated with entries in the photo log.

It is recommended that a form, such as the one on the next page, be used at the time photographs are taken. One form is used for each roll of film. The photographer records the equipment and film used as well as the lighting method that will be used for most of the photographs on that roll (e.g., electronic flash). The photographer then records a brief description of each photograph and the date and time of the photograph. A note is recorded when the photographer changes to a different lens (such as a wide angle lens for overview photographs), changes light source or uses a technique that should be explained (e.g., camera at ground level).

It is not necessary to record f/stops or shutter speeds on the photo log. Such detail is not required for court. However, if the photographer is attempting a new technique, testing new equipment, or just learning the basics of photography, it is important to record additional details about each photograph, including f/stop and shutter speed, in order to learn from each new type of photographic technique or situation. These additional notations can be recorded in another notebook. By looking at the photograph and the notes the photographer can determine what adjustments need to be taken for similar photographs in the future.

Figure 3.2 Photo Log

PHOTOGRAPHIC REPORT	Case number	Scene no.
	Film roll no.	Page
Date:	Location:	
Make and model camera, lens:		
Film type and ISO:	Light source:	

	Description of Photograph	Lens, light source (if different from above), filter, unusual angle, etc.	Time
1			
2			
3			
4			
5			
6			
7			
8			
9			
10			
11			
12			
13			
14			
15			
15			
17			
18			
19			
20			
21			
22			
23			
24			
25			
26			
27			
28			
29			
30			
31			
32			
33			
34			
35			
36			

Photographer:	Approved:	Date:

Using Video to Record the Crime Scene

Videotaping is valuable for showing an overview of the crime scene and should be used in major cases. While video cannot replace still photographs due to its lower resolution, videotaping does provide an easily understandable viewing medium that shows the layout of crime scene and the location of evidence. Videotapes of crime scenes are not often used in court, but they are valuable illustrations for explaining the scene to other investigators and are often used to refresh the memory of those who were involved in processing the crime scene.

Videotapes are considered evidence. You should record only one scene on a videotape and the original videotape should not be edited.

Crime Scene Videotaping Techniques

When videotaping crime scenes, start the videotape with a brief introduction presented by an investigator. The introduction should include the date, time, location, type of crime scene, and any other important introductory information. The introduction should also include a brief description of the rooms and evidence that will be viewed in the videotape. The investigator may want to use a basic diagram as an illustration during the introduction.

Following the introduction the recording is paused and the microphone is turned off. This will prevent any distracting sounds from recording on the videotape during the taping of the scene.

Videotape the crime scene, after the introduction, without any audio recording.

Begin video taping the crime scene with a general overview of the scene and surrounding area. Continue throughout the scene using wide-angle and close up views to show the layout of the scene, location of evidence, and the relevance of evidence within the crime scene. While videotaping, use slow camera movements such as panning, and zooming.

TOOLS OF THE TRADE

Crime Scene Photography Kit

Typical Photo Kit

- Camera
  Most crime scene photographers use a 35mm camera or a high quality digital camera. Digital cameras that have four mega pixel, or greater, image sensors and manual exposure settings (in addition to any automatic or programmed exposure modes) are usually suitable for crime scene and evidence photography.

- Normal lens
  A normal lens provides the best perspective for most photographs. A 50mm lens is considered a normal lens for a 35mm camera.

- Wide-angle lens
  A wide-angle lens is needed when photographing small rooms or other space-constricted areas. A 28mm lens is considered a wide-angle lens for a 35mm camera.

- Close-up lens or accessories
  Most normal lenses do not focus closer than about three feet. A macro lens or a close-up accessory for the normal lens is needed to photograph small items of evidence. Close-up accessories include 1:1 adapters, extension tubes, bellows, reversing rings, or close-up filters.

- Filters

  A polarizing filter is often needed for photographing through glass and into water. Colored filters (red, orange, yellow, blue, and green) are useful when photographing certain types of evidence with black-and-white film.

- Electronic flash

  Electronic flash provides additional light that is often needed when photographing indoors, outdoors at night, filling in shadows in bright daylight scenes and for lighting evidence.

- Remote sync cord for electronic flash

  A remote sync cord allows the electronic flash to be operated when it is not mounted on camera. Many photographs, especially photographs certain types of evidence, cannot be photographed with the flash mounted on the camera.

- Extra camera and electronic flash batteries

  Batteries can expire without warning during the documentation of a scene. Extra batteries for both the camera and electronic flash should be included in the camera kit.

- Locking cable release

  A locking cable release is used to lock open the camera's shutter during long exposures and when using the "painting with light" technique for photographing large nighttime scenes. Cameras that have a built-in feature that locks open the shutter do not require a locking cable release.

- Tripod

  A tripods is necessary to steady the camera for long exposures and for positioning the camera during certain types of evidence photography.

- Film

  Medium speed (ISO 100 or 200) color print film is most often used for crime scene photography. Black-and-white film is used for certain types of evidence photography.

- Operation manuals for camera, electronic flash and accessories

  Equipment operating manuals should be carried in the field for reference. With the many features on modern cameras and electronic flash units, it may be necessary to refer to the manuals for specialized photographic techniques.

- Photo log, notebook and pen
  A photo log is necessary for recording information about each photograph taken at a crime scene. A notebook is valuable for recording other notes during the investigation.

- Scales and tape measure
  A variety of scales, including 6" and 36" sizes, must be available for photographing different types of subjects. Long tape measures with large numbers are sometimes necessary when photographing large items of evidence or large areas in a crime scene.

- ABFO #2 scale
  The ABFO #2 scale is the preferred scale for photographing injuries.

- Angle-finder
  An angle-finder is used to help position a camera for photographing certain types of evidence at the crime scene.

- Color chart or color control patches
  Color chart or color control patches are useful as color references in injury photography

- 18 percent gray card
  The 18 percent gray card is used as an aid in getting accurate exposures.

- Index cards and felt pen
  When a number or other identifier is needed in a photograph, simply write the number or identifier on an index card and place it in the photograph.

- Flashlight
  A flashlight not only helps you see in dark areas, but it is useful for previewing lighting during evidence photography. By shining the light on evidence from different angles you can see where it is best to position the electronic flash for a photograph.

Other Equipment to Consider

- Telephoto lenses
  While telephoto lenses are seldom used in crime scene photography, they are necessary for most types of surveillance photography.

- Supplementary light meter
  Supplementary light meters are usually more effective than the metering system inside the camera and are most useful for low light level readings, such as ambient light photography at night.

- Small tools
  Small tools are helpful when emergency camera repairs must be done in the field.

- Devices for positioning evidence and scales
  Blocks of wood, clothes pins, clamps and other devices can be used for positioning evidence and scales for close-up photography.

- White handkerchief or other flash diffusion material
  A white handkerchief or similar material can be placed over the head of an electronic flash unit to reduce the intensity of the flash.

Scales and Measuring Devices

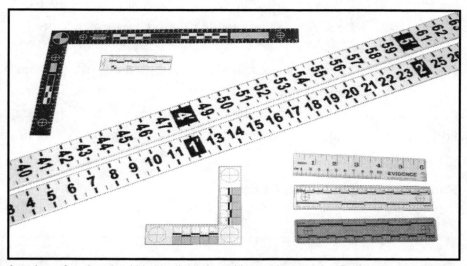

A variety of scales should be available for evidence photography. Evidence scales include "L" shaped scales for footwear impressions, the ABFO #2 scale (bottom-center of illustration) for injuries, six inch scales for small evidence, and 36-inch scales for tire impressions, vehicle collision damage and bloodstain photography.

Scales and measuring devices are frequently used in crime scene and evidence photographs. While scales are sometimes used to orient the viewer of the photograph to the relative size of the object in the photograph, they are primarily used to serve as a basis for making enlargements to a specified magnification level, such as life size. This is critical for photographs of evidence that later will become the basis for a comparison—such as a photograph of a footwear impression that will be compared with the shoe of a suspect—since a photograph must be printed to life size. A variety of scales must be available for photographing different types of subjects.

- Small self-adhesive scales are used to photograph evidence such as fingerprints and bullet holes on walls.

- Six-inch scales are used for photographing most small to medium sized evidence. Some six-inch scales have small numbers for extreme close-up photographs and others have large numbers for photographing larger items. The larger numbers allow easy reading of the scale from a greater distance.

- Large "L" shaped scales are frequently used for photographing footwear impression evidence while small "L" shaped scales are used for photographing injuries such as bruises and bite marks.

- Longer scales with large, easy-to-read numbers are used for photographing tire tread impressions and bloodstain scenes. These long scales can be metal or cloth tape measures or plastic scales.

When using scales in photographs, two photographs of each item of evidence must be taken. One photograph must be taken without the scale in view and one photograph taken with the scale. The first photograph will document that the photographer did not cover or block other evidence with the scale.

Numbering and Directional Devices

Numbering devices are commonly used to identify similar appearing evidence. Directional devices, most commonly in the form of an arrow, are sometimes placed in photographs to indicate a direction.

Numbering devices are commonly used to identify similar appearing evidence. For example, several bullet holes in a wall would need to be individually numbered. It is usually unnecessary to place numbering devices in a photograph to identify items of evidence that cannot be confused with other items.

When using numbering devices in photographs, two photographs of each view must be taken. One photograph must be taken without the numbering device in view and one photograph taken with the numbering device. The first photograph will document that the photographer did not cover or block other evidence with the numbering device.

Directional devices, most commonly in the form of an arrow, are sometimes placed in photographs to indicate a direction. The direction could be "up" (e.g., fingerprints on a vertical surface) or "north" (e.g., footwear impressions). This helps to show orientation of evidence when the photograph is viewed.

When using directional devices in photographs, two photographs of each view must be taken. One photograph must be taken without the directional device in view and one photograph taken with the directional device. The first photograph will document that the photographer did not cover or block other evidence with the directional device.

SUMMARY

As a member of the crime scene investigation team, the crime scene photographer has a crucial role in documenting the crime scene and its evidence. The photographer must not only know how to take quality photographs, but must know when to take photographs during the different stages of the crime scene investigation. The photographer must have the tools and supplies necessary to adequately photograph the scene and the various types of evidence that is discovered during the processing of the crime scene.

DISCUSSION QUESTIONS

1. Describe the six steps usually used in the processing of crime scenes.
2. When photographing crime scenes located inside a building, what should the exterior photographs include?
3. Give an example of a crime scene in which aerial photography may be useful.
4. In aerial photography, why should you use a zoom lens? Fast shutter speeds?

5. When photographing an interior space, what should be the first photograph taken?

6. What type of lens is usually used for overview photographs in rooms?

7. What is a crime scene diagram? What information should it contain?

8. How can photography be used to test a theory based on a statement given by a suspect, witness or victim?

9. Describe the role of the Crime Scene Photographer.

10. Other than a camera, what equipment should a Crime Scene Photographer have on hand to photograph crime scenes?

ADDITIONAL RESOURCES

Byrd, Mike, (2001) *Crime Scene Evidence: A Guide to the Recovery and Collection of Physical Evidence*, Staggs Publishing, Wildomar, California 92595

Duckworth, John E., (1983) *Forensic Photography*, Charles C. Thomas, Springfield, Illinois 62717

Fisher, Barry A. J., (2003) *Techniques of Crime Scene Investigation*, Seventh Edition, CRC Press, Boca Raton, Florida 33431

Miller, Larry S., (1998) *Police Photography*, Fourth Edition, Anderson Publishing Co., Cincinnati, Ohio 45202

National Institute of Justice, (2000) *Crime Scene Investigation, A Guide for Law Enforcement*, U.S. Department of Justice, Office of Justice Programs, Washington, DC 20531

Staggs, Steven, (2005) *Crime Scene and Evidence Photographer's Guide*, Second Edition, Staggs Publishing, Wildomar, California 92595

Chapter 4

Crimes Against Persons

OVERVIEW

The results of crimes committed against people, including homicides and assaults, are vividly, and many times graphically, recorded with photography. These photographs can be extremely valuable in explaining such crimes as well as the brutality of these offenses.

OBJECTIVES

In this chapter, you will learn how to photograph crime scenes and subjects involving:

1. Injuries
2. Assault
3. Homicide
4. Suicide
5. Autopsy

INTRODUCTION TO CRIMES AGAINST PERSONS PHOTOGRAPHY

Each crime scene has unique characteristics. The type of photographs needed for complete documentation will be determined at the scene by the investigators familiar with the crime. While this chapter includes suggestions for taking some of the common types of photographs of certain subjects and at certain scenes, they should not be considered comprehensive lists of all the photographs needed in every case.

When you arrive at the scene, be sure to have the lead investigator give you a walk through of the scene to point out evidence and other aspects of the crime scene that should be photographed.

PHOTOGRAPHING INJURIES

In addition to photographically documenting the location where the crime occurred, the body of the victim can be considered a crime scene in itself. Injuries must be documented in a thorough, detailed manner.

Injuries are referred to by their type. When discussing injuries with other investigators, medical personnel, and in court, and when documenting injuries in notes and reports, it is important to refer to injuries by their type. Figure 4.1 lists the common types of injury and their descriptions.

Figure 4.1 Definitions of Injury Types

Abrasion
A rubbing away of upper skin layers, a forceful rubbing or scraping against another object (e.g., "road rash" or rope burn).

Avulsion
Tissue separated by force, a tearing away from a part.

Bite mark
Puncture or contusion received from human or animal teeth, or from an insect.

Figure 4.1 Definitions of Injury Types (cont'd)

Bruise

Impact injury causing superficial hematoma (bleeding) underneath upper skin layers.

Contusion

Injury in which skin is not broken but traumatized with injury to underlying structure.

Defense wound

Wound received in protecting self from an assailant.

Incision

A precise cut to the skin with a sharp or surgical instrument.

Laceration

Skin tissue cut by a dull or blunt object appearing torn or mangled.

Puncture

Injury from a slender sharp pointed object causing a hole-like wound (e.g., nail, ice pick, or teeth).

Usually a victim's injuries heal over time, and by the time a case goes to trial the victim may have completely healed. Alternatively, the injuries suffered by the victim may have been fatal. In either case, photographs are essential in the trial of the accused so the court and jury can see the extent of the injuries that were inflicted on the victim.

The following information on photographing injuries will apply to most injuries including cuts, bruises, bite marks and gunshot wounds.

Equipment for Photographing Injuries

When photographing injuries, use color film. Do not use any type of filter, other than close-up filters, over the camera's lens. This is because many filters can affect the colors in a photograph. Color charts can be placed in photographs so that when prints of the injury photographs are made, the colors in the photographs can be printed accurately. Some experts can testify to the age of an injury because of its color, or can testify that the differing colors of two injuries indicate they were not made at the same time.

A scale must be used in the close-up photograph. An ABFO #2 scale is the scale used most often for photographs of injuries.

Electronic flash should be used for injury photographs. This is because daylight color print film is color balanced for daylight, electronic flash, and blue flash bulbs. The use of any other lighting sources will result in photographs with incorrect colors. The electronic flash should be diffused, either with a wide-angle diffuser or a handkerchief placed over the head of the flash. A ring light flash can also be used for injury photography.

A macro lens or some type of close-up accessory will be needed for close-up photographs of most injuries. This is because normal lenses are designed to focus from about three feet to infinity and therefore cannot focus close enough to record most injuries. To record fine detail when photographing evidence, the injury should fill the frame of the camera's viewfinder.

Basic techniques in photographing injuries

When photographing injuries on a body, it is important to remember to identify the body on which the injury is located. The first photograph taken in the series of injury photographs is a photograph of the victim's face. This will identify the individual who sustained the injury. This is necessary because there have been cases in court where an opposing attorney has challenged injury photographs because it was unclear who the injuries in the photographs belonged to.

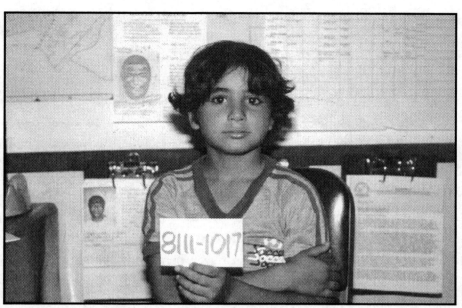

Photograph the victim's face in the first photograph in the series. Do not, however, have a cluttered or distracting background as in this photograph.

Do not have distracting backgrounds in the photographs when photographing injury victims. When the photographs are displayed in court, jurors may become distracted by the things that appear in the background. Photograph victims with a blank wall, curtain, or a neutral backdrop behind them. Some crime scene photographers carry white and black pieces of cloth to use as backdrops.

After photographing the face of the victim, photograph the area of the body that includes the injury so that the location of the injury can clearly be identified. For example, if the injury is a bruise on a victim's upper right arm, photograph enough of the upper right arm so the area shown in the photograph is identifiable as an upper right arm. If photographed too close, the area might not be clearly identifiable and could be mistaken for another part of the body.

Next, take a close-up photograph of the injury. A scale must be used in the close-up photograph. An ABFO #2 scale is the scale used most often for photographs of injuries that may be compared with an instrument suspected of causing the injury (handprint, belt buckle, teeth, etc.). The scale must be placed on the same plane as the injury and the camera oriented so the film plane is parallel to the injury.

Focus carefully. When taking close-up photographs one of the most common problems encountered is shallow depth-of-field. Therefore, accurate focusing is critical. One important technique regarding focusing for injury photography is to avoid focusing on the scale. Instead, be sure to focus on the evidence. While it is frequently easier to focus on the markings or edge of the scale, the scale may not always be on the exact plane of the injury. It is better to have a sharp image of the injury and a slightly out of focus scale than to have a sharp image of the scale and the injury out of focus.

If you are hand-holding the camera while taking a close-up photograph of an injury, you should first rough-size (scale) the injury by focusing with the lens-focusing ring. When you have the injury just about focused in your viewfinder, stop focusing the lens with the focusing ring. Then you can fine-focus on the injury by moving the camera in and out. While maintaining the fine-focus by moving the camera in and out slightly, lightly depress the shutter button to take the photograph.

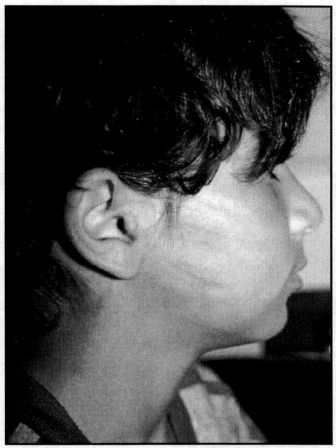

Injury, handprint from a slap, photographed with oblique lighting from a diffused electronic flash.

Lighting is usually provided by an electronic flash. A small electronic flash with a wide-angle diffuser or white handkerchief over the flash head works well. When using a small (low power) electronic flash it is often possible to mount the flash on top of the camera and achieve satisfactory results. With flash units that are more powerful, it is likely the flash will wash out detail due to the intensity of the flash. In this case, you will have to remove the flash from the camera and position it further away from the injury to prevent washing out detail. Lighting injuries requires practice to find the best combinations of flash units and flash distances for the best results.

Continue by photographing all the remaining injuries. If there are multiple injuries, it may be necessary to number them in the photographs, to clearly identify each one. An adhesive number, or an adhesive label with a number written on it, can be placed near each injury and included in the photograph for identification purposes.

Be sure to photograph any old scars and fading bruises that you notice. These may be signs of previous injuries, which may indicate a pattern of abuse over time.

When necessary, take additional photographs 24 to 48 hours after the offense when the coloring and size of the victim's bruises become more visible.

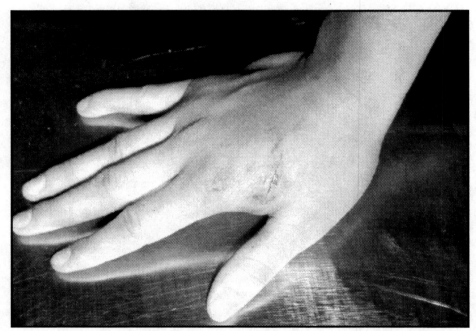

Knife wound on a suspect's hand photographed to document his involvement in an assault with a deadly weapon.

Ultraviolet lighting techniques can be used to produce high-resolution photographs of skin surfaces. It is a good technique for photographing bite marks, cuts, and scratches. Bruises with blood accumulation close to the skin surface can also be photographed with ultraviolet photography.

To photograph using ultraviolet light you will need a camera, high speed black-and-white film, a Kodak Wratten 18A filter, and a lens capable of transmitting light between 320nm and 400nm. A light source rich in ultraviolet light is necessary. Such light sources include tungsten lights, photoflood lights, fluorescent lights and electronic flash.

A Kodak Wratten 18A filter is placed over the camera's lens during the exposure. The 18A filter blocks visible light while allowing ultraviolet light to pass through. Exposure settings are determined by evaluating test photographs. You can find a starting point for exposures by using the exposure settings indicated by the camera's internal exposure meter with the filter in place or with an external exposure meter using a filter factor of 80 (+6.5 stops). Exposures should be bracketed by two f/stops.

When taking ultraviolet photographs, use an ultraviolet ABFO #2 scale. Also, be sure to take both white light and ultraviolet light photographs of the injury. These can be used for comparison and for explaining your technique in court.

Bite Marks

Usually, photographs are the only means available for an expert in forensic odontology to evaluate bite marks. Bite marks should be carefully photographed using the equipment and techniques described above. The ABFO #2 scale should be used for bite mark photography.

ASSAULT SCENES

Assault scenes, from sexual assault to domestic violence cases, usually consist of two primary subjects for photography, the victim and the crime scene. In some cases a third subject must be photographed, the suspect. Whenever possible, all three should be photographed to document the crime.

When photographing victims of assault it is important to photograph all visible injuries using the techniques described earlier. It is also important to photograph any other evidence relating to the victim. This would include the condition of the victim's clothing. The victim's clothing may have been torn, blood-spattered, or stained with semen. If the victim is wearing the clothing when you arrive to document the crime, be sure to photograph the clothing as it appears while worn by the victim. Often, clothing will be collected as evidence, especially in sexual assault cases. The clothing can be photographed in greater detail in the laboratory to document ripped material, semen stains (usually when illuminated with a forensic light source) and other trace evidence.

The location of the crime must be photographed. Photographs can document the appearance of the assault scene including overturned furniture, bloodstain, and other indications of a struggle.

It is usually a good idea to photograph the suspect, if the suspect can be located. An assault suspect frequently will have received injuries from the victim during the assault. Scratch marks, bite marks, and cut or bruised knuckles are a few examples of injuries that can be observed on suspects. A suspect may also have bloodstain on them as well as torn clothing and trace evidence, such as hair, from the victim. All injuries on a suspect should be documented using the techniques described earlier.

There have been numerous cases where a victim has described a physical characteristic that would help to identify the suspect, such as a birthmark or mole. If you locate the suspect, be sure to photograph the presence or absence of such characteristics described by the victim. This will assist the investigation by either identifying or exonerating the suspect.

HOMICIDE

When photographing a homicide, take a series of photographs that will help other investigators, the District Attorney and perhaps a jury understand where and how the crime was committed. These photographs can also be used to recreate the crime and to prove or disprove a theory or a suspect's explanation.

Homicide Scene

Be sure to use color film when photographing homicide scenes, and to switch to black-and-white film as necessary to photograph certain evidence, such as fingerprints and impressions. You usually have just one opportunity to photograph a homicide scene, so it is best to be thorough. When in doubt, take extra photographs. In a significant case, such as a homicide, it is better to be criticized for taking too many photographs than for missing any important ones.

Photographs to Consider

When photographing a homicide inside a building, such as a residence, photographs should include the exterior of the building including all sides of the building, all doors, windows, and other means of entrance or exit, and escape routes. Consider photographing the general neighborhood, street, and vehicles. In some cases, aerial photographs may provide valuable perspectives of the scene.

Photograph any evidence discovered outside the building, such as impressions, signs of forced entry, blood trails, and dropped items.

Photograph the entrance into the scene, the room in which the body was found, and any adjoining rooms, hallways, and stairwells. In residential homicides, you should photograph all the rooms in the residence. These photographs should show any signs of the victim or suspect's activity before the homicide, such as lights on, food cooking, cigarettes in an ash tray, empty beer cans, etc. In addition, any evidence of a struggle, such as overturned furniture or broken items, should be illustrated with photographs.

Photograph the body. Start by photographing the body from as many of the five angles (or views) as are available. The five angles are from both sides of the body, both ends of the body, and overhead (straight down). In many cases, you will not be able to photograph all five angles due to the position of the body. When the body is against a wall, in a closet, or in the trunk of a car you will be limited in the number of angles available for photographs.

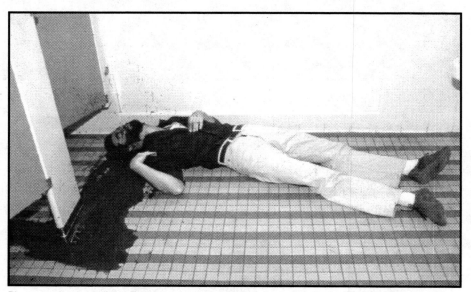

Photograph a body from five angles when available including both sides of the body (due to the position of this body against a wall, only one side of the body could be photographed).

Photographs are also taken from each end of the body.

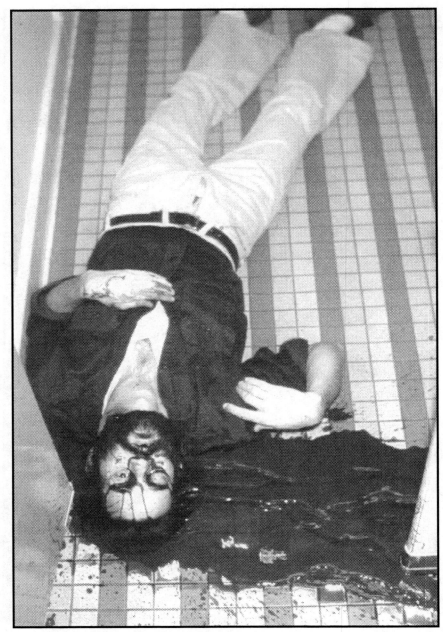

The purpose of this series of photographs to establish the position and condition of the body.

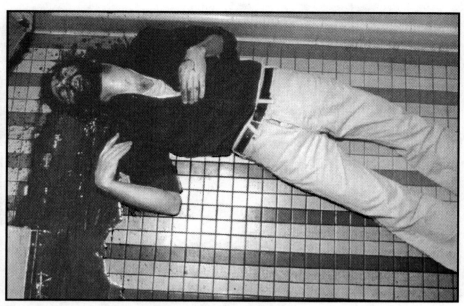

Photographs are taken from above the body.

After photographing the five angles, you should photograph body wounds and injuries that are visible. Take two photographs of each body wound, the first to show the location of the wound on the body and second to show the detail (with a close-up photograph) of the wound. This is not usually a time to take photographs with scales, because more detailed photographs using scales will be taken at the autopsy. You just want to document the presence of the wounds in photographs of the body at the scene.

At some point, the body will be removed from the homicide scene. Be certain to photograph the area under the body after the body is moved.

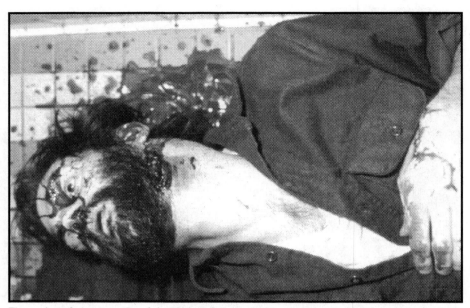

The series of photographs of the body is followed with more detailed, closer views to show injuries and other related evidence.

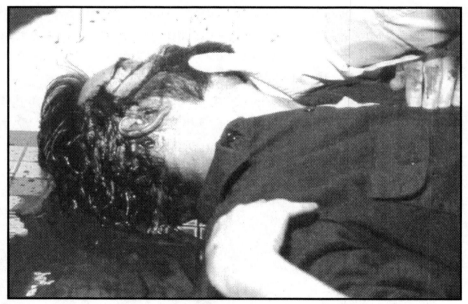

Photograph of a hammer wound located behind the victim's right ear.

Photograph any weapons found at the crime scene. If the weapon and body can be included in one view, take photographs to show the location of the weapon in relation to the body. If there are bullet holes in walls or other objects at the scene, photograph them using at least two photographs. One photograph must show the location of the bullet hole and a second photograph showing a close-up of the bullet hole (include a scale). If you have multiple bullet holes, be sure to number them with adhesive numbers or adhesive labels with numbers written on them.

Photograph trace evidence, such as bloodstain, fingerprints, and footprints in dust or blood. When photographing fingerprints and impressions use black-and-white film. Black-and-white film provides more contrast than color film and will show more detail in the evidence.

While photographing the homicide scene, you should be aware of the theories under consideration by investigators. Many times theories can be tested through photography. One example is the view of suspects, witnesses, or victims during the homicide. You can place the camera at a subject's viewing position and, using a 35mm lens, demonstrate what the subject could have seen.

SUICIDE

Suicide scenes should be photographed much the same as homicides. Some photographers will do a less-than-thorough job of photographing a scene if it appears to be a suicide. However, in some cases it may take weeks to determine if a death was, in fact, a suicide. If the case should turn out to be a homicide, and you photographed it as thoroughly as a homicide, you should have the photographs necessary for an effective investigation.

Hanging

When photographing a suspected hanging suicide the body must be photographed from several different angles to show the location and position of the body. Photograph the hanging device (e.g., rope) any knots, and how and to what it was fastened. Photograph any visible injuries including injuries to the victim's neck.

Photograph the location where the victim was located and anything that would indicate the death is a suicide. Photograph doors and windows locked from inside, a kicked over chair, suicide note, etc.

Gunshot Suicide

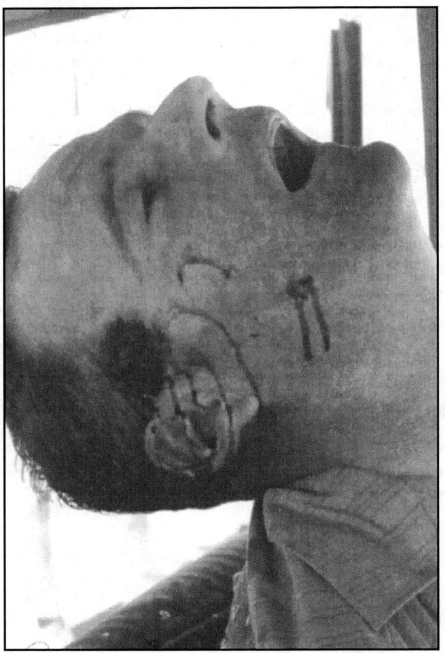

Photograph gunshot entrance and exit wounds on the bodies of suicide victims.

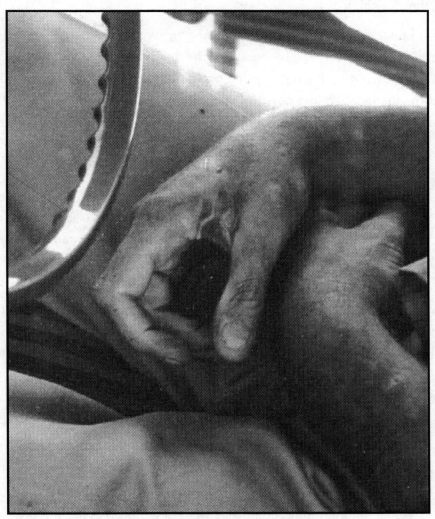

Photograph gunshot residue on the hands of suicide victims. Note on the victim's hand the pattern of the hammer from the revolver used in the suicide.

When photographing a suspected gunshot suicide photograph the location where the victim was located and anything that would indicate the death is a suicide. Photograph doors and windows locked from inside, suicide notes, etc.

Photograph the body from several different angles to show the location and position of the body. Photograph the gunshot entrance and exit wounds, soot or tattooing at entrance wounds, and gunshot residue on the victim's hands.

Photograph the weapon and its location. Also, include photographs that show position of weapon in relation to the body.

Other Suicides

Other suicides, such as intentional drug overdoses and jumping from buildings, should be photographed in much the same manner as the examples above. Photograph the body from several different angles to show the location and position of the body. Empty prescription bottles, suicide notes, and other indications that the death was a suicide should also be photographed.

AUTOPSY

Photographs are normally taken at autopsies to document the condition of the body and support the findings (cause and manner of death) of the medical examiner or forensic pathologist.

The investigating agency is usually encouraged, or even required, to attend the autopsy to exchange information with the medical examiner or pathologist. Most medical examiners and pathologists, or members of their staff, take photographs at the autopsy. However, the investigating agency may be allowed to take additional photographs during the autopsy.

When photographing an autopsy, be sure to follow any protocols required by the medical examiner or forensic pathologist. Protocols may include protective gear worn by the photographer and decontamination procedures.

When photographing autopsies use color film. Do not use any type of filter, other than close-up filters, over the camera's lens. A scale must be used in many of the close-up photographs taken at autopsies. Standard six-inch scales and ABFO #2 scales are used in photographs of autopsies.

Electronic flash should be used for autopsy photographs. Either the electronic flash should be diffused, with a wide-angle diffuser or a handkerchief placed over the head of the flash. A ring light flash can also be used for injury photography.

A macro lens or some type of close-up accessory will be needed for close-up photographs of most injuries. Specialized medical lenses are available but they are usually very expensive.

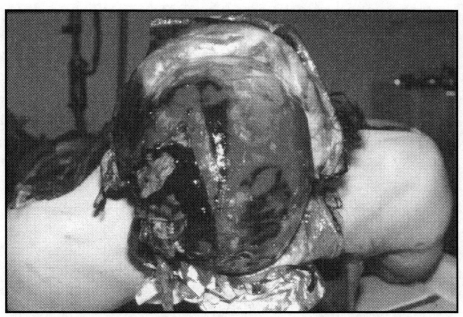

Photograph taken into the skull to show injuries sustained in a beating with a hammer.

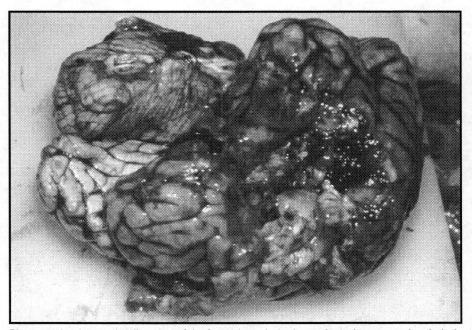

Photograph taken at the direction of the forensic pathologist to show damage to the victim's brain.

Photographing autopsies is done much like photographing injuries on other victims. Many of the photographs you take will be directed by the medical examiner or forensic pathologist (e.g., damage to a body organ). Other photographs are considered standard views. These standard views include overview photographs of the body before the body is unclothed or cleaned-up, tattoos, marks and scars (include a scale) and any other identifying photographs. In addition, it is important to photograph all surfaces of the body to also indicate where there is an absence of wounds (e.g., the victim was not shot in the back).

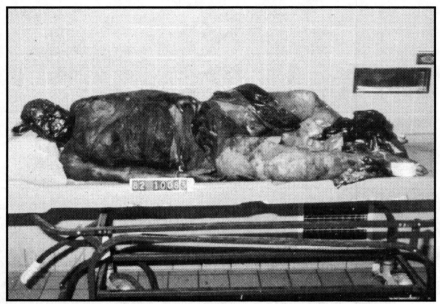

Overall photographs of the body before the body is unclothed or cleaned up.

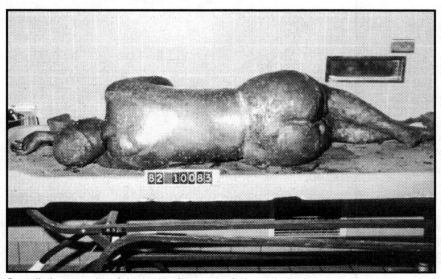

Overall photographs of the body after the body is unclothed.

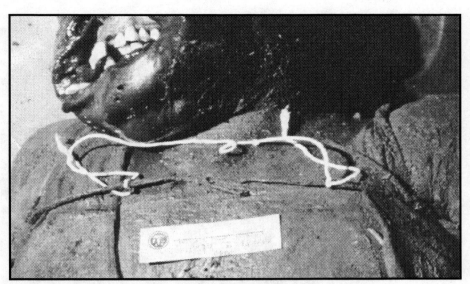
Knots tied in bindings on the victim are photographed.

Photograph gunshot wounds, any visible pattern of gunshot residue and the victim's hands if there is any gunshot residue (include a scale).

Take close-up photographs of the injuries. A scale must be used in close-up photographs. An ABFO #2 scale is the scale used most often for photographs of injuries that may be compared with an instrument suspected of causing the injury (handprint, belt buckle, teeth, etc.). The scale must be placed on the same plane as the injury and the camera oriented so the film plane is parallel to the injury.

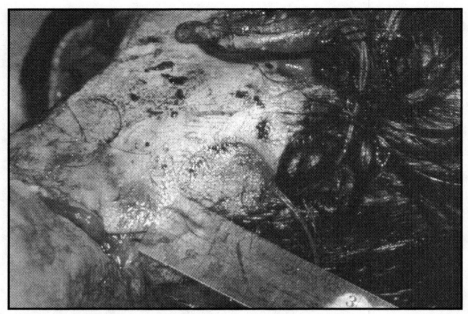

Autopsy photograph — close-up of neck wound caused by a hammer.

Focus carefully. When taking close-up photographs one of the most common problems encountered is shallow depth-of-field. Therefore, accurate focusing is critical.

If you are hand holding the camera while taking a close-up photograph of an injury you should first rough size (scale) the injury by focusing with the lens-focusing ring. When you have the injury just about focused in your viewfinder stop focusing the lens with the focusing ring. Then you can fine focus the injury by moving the camera in and out from the subject. While maintaining the fine focus by moving the camera in and out slightly, lightly depress the shutter button to take the photograph.

SUMMARY

Most "crimes against persons" involve injuries. By utilizing the simple concepts and steps discussed in this chapter, most injuries can be documented to further the investigation and, in many cases, inform the jury.

DISCUSSION QUESTIONS

1. Why is it important to have photos of a victims injuries?

2. What photo should be taken first when photographing injuries? Why?

3. If you are hand-holding the camera while taking a close-up photo of an injury, how should you focus?

4. Should you photograph any old scars or fading bruises? Why?

5. What are the three subjects at an assault scene that should be photographed whenever possible?

6. How should you start when photographing a body in a homicide scene?

7. Assuming there are multiple bullet holes, what do you do?

8. Why is it important to be just as thorough with a suspected suicide case as a homicide case?

9. Are photos normally taken at autopsies? Why?

10. What types of scales are used in photos of autopsies?

EXERCISES and ACTIVITIES

Disclaimer: Under no circumstance are students supposed to create actual defects upon themselves or others for the purpose of this course. No permanent markers should be used; make-up that can be washed off is preferred.

1. Have the students, using washable ink pen, felt-tip marker, or make-up, draw a defect on their own body. Then without any discussion, have them photograph the defect on another student. Then put the camera away until later in the lecture.

2. After the lecture, go over the students' pictures with the class and analyze the pictures as necessary.

3. Photograph a location from two different aspects showing how important the composition of the photograph is.

4. Research the title given to a crime scene photographer in a local law enforcement agency.

5. Research on the Internet the photographs of the O.J. Simpson case and formulate a one-page plan of the initial photographs needed of the scene.

ADDITIONAL RESOURCES

Bowers, C. Michael, (2004) *Forensic Dental Evidence: An Investigator's Handbook*, Elsevier Academic Press, San Diego, California 92101

Byrd, Mike, (2001) *Crime Scene Evidence: A Guide to the Recovery and Collection of Physical Evidence*, Staggs Publishing, Wildomar, California 92595

Dorion, Robert B.J., (2004) *Bitemark Evidence*, CRC Press, Boca Raton, Florida 33431

Duckworth, John E., (1983) *Forensic Photography*, Charles C. Thomas, Springfield, Illinois 62717

Fisher, Barry A. J., (2003) *Techniques of Crime Scene Investigation,* Seventh Edition, CRC Press, Boca Raton, Florida 33431

Gibson, H. L., (1973) *Medical Photography: Clinical—Ultraviolet—Infrared*, Eastman Kodak Company, Rochester, New York 14650

McDonald, James A., (1992) *Close-up and Macro Photography for Evidence Technicians*, Second Edition, Phototext Books, Palatine, Illinois 60067

Miller, Larry S., (1998) *Police Photography,* Fourth Edition, Anderson Publishing Co., Cincinnati, Ohio 45202

Staggs, Steven, (2005) *Crime Scene and Evidence Photographer's Guide,* Second Edition, Staggs Publishing, Wildomar, California 92595

Chapter 5

Crimes Against Property

OVERVIEW

Photographs are not only valuable in documenting property crime scenes, but are very effective for showing the elements of crimes. Photographs can show the *res gestae* (the full story of the crime), the *corpus delicti* (the body of the crime), and the *modus operandi* (the method of the crime). Photographs that illustrate these points can be extremely valuable for the investigation and later when presenting the case in court.

OBJECTIVES

In this chapter, you will learn how to photograph crime scenes involving:
1. Burglary
2. Robbery
3. Arson
4. Explosions

INTRODUCTION TO CRIMES AGAINST PROPERTY PHOTOGRAPHY

Each crime scene has unique characteristics. The type of photographs needed for complete documentation will be determined at the scene by the investigators familiar with the crime. While this chapter includes suggestions for taking some of the common types of photographs taken at certain scenes, they should not be considered comprehensive lists of all the photographs needed in every case.

When you arrive at the scene, be sure to have the lead investigator give you a walk through of the scene to point out evidence and other aspects of the crime scene that should be photographed.

RESIDENTIAL AND COMMERCIAL BURGLARY SCENES

Photographs of burglary scenes will normally be taken with color film. However, some types of evidence should be photographed with black-and-white film. Black-and-white film has more contrast and can bring out more detail in some types of evidence. Examples of evidence that should be photographed close-up with black-and-white film include fingerprints, tool marks, and footwear impressions.

The series of photographs taken at residential or commercial burglary scenes should begin with photographs of the exterior areas of the building. Many crime scene photographers will go to the nearest intersection and photograph the street signs to identify the name of the street on which the building is located. A photograph of the street number on the building will help to further identify its exact location. If the building has an identifying sign, such as a business name, it should also appear in a photograph. It may be useful to take a few photographs that show the general location of the building. This may be accomplished in a residential burglary by photographing the residence from a distance so the houses on either side of the residence are also in view. Consider photographing the vehicles parked on the street. There have been cases where the suspect's vehicle was abandoned when the suspect fled the scene. If an escape route can be identified, a series of photographs should be taken to illustrate how the suspect escaped from the scene.

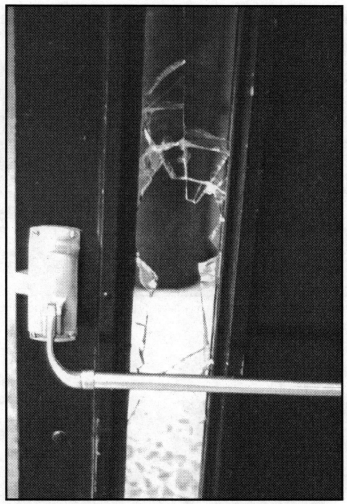

Photographs illustrate the elements of the crime. In this case, a suspect broke the glass and pulled the crash bar to open the door.

Any evidence discovered outside the building should be photographed. This would include tire impressions on driveways, footwear impressions in flowerbeds, pry marks on window screens, stolen property or burglary tools dropped or abandoned by the suspect, etc.

Next, if the point of entry into the building can be located, photograph the point of entry with mid-range and close-up views from both the exterior and interior of the building.

The following illustrations demonstrate how a series of photographs can be taken to clearly show how the suspects entered an office building during a burglary.

A series of photographs of this commercial burglary includes a view of the front of the office building.

The next photograph takes us around the side of the office building to an attached warehouse.

A mid-range photograph is taken to show the area of the point of entry into the warehouse.

Point of entry into warehouse, exterior view.

Point of entry into warehouse, interior view.

This view shows the point of entry into the warehouse in the foreground, and the point of entry from the warehouse into the office building in the background.

Burglary tools left by suspects outside the final point of entry.

Photograph of the area around the point of entry in the office building.

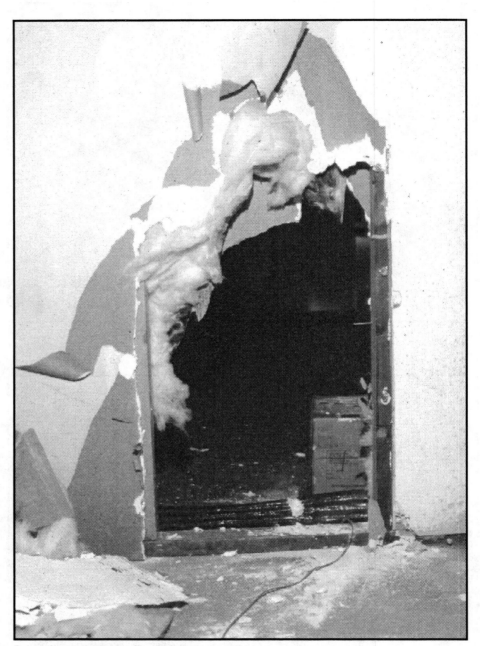

Point of entry into the office building.

Point of entry viewed from the inside of the office building.

Interior photographs are taken next. Each room of the residence or commercial building that appears to have been disturbed should be photographed. For each room or area begin with a view of the entrance. Photograph the room or area, as it appears when you first step inside. Take overview photographs from each corner of the room to show the layout of the room. A wide-angle lens is usually used for interior overview photographs. In large rooms you may need to take additional photographs from other locations for complete coverage.

These overview photographs, along with mid-range photographs, should also show things disturbed by the suspect (e.g., moved furniture) as well as the positions of any potential items of evidence. If the overview photographs do not show the location of a specific item of evidence, take a mid-range photograph or an additional overview photograph from another angle to show the location of the evidence. Continue with photographs of other rooms connected with the crime scene.

This photograph shows the area where a computer was removed and damage to the desk (the computer had been locked down to the desk).

Photograph the evidence that is discovered inside the building. Photograph damage to locks, doors and safes. Tool marks and trace evidence such as burned matches, cigarette butts and bloodstain should also be photographed. Fingerprints and dusty footwear prints on floors can be photographed before they are collected.

Sometimes a suspect may flee before completing the burglary. Photograph burglary tools left behind by the suspect or victim's property stacked at a door.

ROBBERY SCENES

Robbery scenes, including home invasion robberies, should be thoroughly documented with photographs. The location of the scene should be photographed. If the crime occurred outdoors, the area should be photographed with a series of photographs by beginning from the outside of the scene and working in toward the location of the robbery.

If the robbery occurred indoors, the exterior of the building should be photographed and then the interior. The room, or rooms, in which the crime occurred, should be photographed with overview photographs from each corner of the room to show the layout of the room. A wide-angle lens is usually used for interior overview photographs. In large rooms you may need to take additional photographs from other locations for complete coverage.

Evidence should be photographed with mid-range photographs to show the location of the evidence in the scene and with close-up photographs to show the detail of the evidence. Evidence might include robbery notes, fingerprints, dusty footwear impressions, and duct tape or rope to bind victims.

With robbery scenes, you will usually have a victim or witnesses that can describe the actions taken by the suspect. Photograph anything that helps to illustrate what happened during the crime. Photograph the suspect's approach and escape routes. Consider taking photographs that illustrate the view victims and witnesses had during the incident. You can place the camera at a subject's viewing position and, using a 35mm lens, demonstrate what the subject could have seen.

If the robbery occurred in an area protected with video surveillance, the surveillance videotape should be taken into evidence.

If victims or witnesses have been injured in the robbery, be sure to photograph their injuries. Chapter 4 includes information on photographing injuries.

ARSON AND FIRE SCENES

Buildings

Arson and fire scenes present challenges not encountered at most other scenes. These challenges include avoiding personal injury while working in damaged structures, protecting camera equipment from water damage, providing adequate lighting for photography, and identifying what needs to be photographed.

Color film should be used for fire and arson photography. Color film is necessary to show subtle color variations between objects and smoke stains.

If possible, photographs should be taken during a structure fire to show the progression of the fire, and color of smoke and flame.

If possible, photographs should be taken during a structure fire. These photographs can show the presence or absence of steam or smoke and the color of flame. The color of smoke can help identify what material may have burned and the presence of an accelerant. The color of flame can indicate the type of materials burning and the temperature (intensity) of the fire.

Photographs should be taken of parked vehicles in the area and bystanders watching the fire. It is not uncommon for an arsonist to return to the area to watch the fire burn.

Once the fire has been extinguished an investigation can begin. Photography of the scene should be done as soon as possible to document the condition of the structure and the presence and appearance of evidence before the scene is disturbed or altered. However, safety should be considered before beginning photography, especially inside the structure. Burned structures may be in danger of collapse and materials or chemicals inside the building may pose a health hazard. Be certain the building is safe before you enter the building. You should wear protective equipment, including head protection, when inside the building. Camera equipment should be protected from dripping water. Some arson photographers will cover their camera with plastic, while others will have an assistant hold an umbrella to protect their equipment.

Photography should begin with photographs of the exterior of the structure. Photograph all sides of the structure. These photographs should show the extent of the exterior damage and the locations of doors and windows. Photograph smoke, heat and burn patterns on exterior window frames, doors, walls and the roof. Photograph circuit breaker boxes (fuse boxes) to show the position of the switches. Photograph gas meters and chimneys. Photograph any evidence located outside the scene including footwear and tire impressions, empty gasoline cans, and forced entry to the structure.

Consider taking aerial photographs of the scene. If an aircraft is not available you may be able to take photographs from the top of a nearby building or the top of the extended ladder on the fire department's ladder truck. These views will show fire damage that cannot be seen from the sides of the building.

Photograph the exterior of the building to show the extent of fire damage and locations of doors and windows.

Photograph circuit breaker boxes to show the positions of the breaker switches.

The interior of building will be photographed next. One significant challenge in photographing fire damage inside buildings is lighting. The camera records reflected light, but since the charred walls in a fire scene tend to absorb instead of reflect light, photographs are often underexposed. This is a significant problem because underexposed photographs will not record the subtle detail of burn patterns. To compensate for the probable underexposure, you should bracket exposures up to two f/stops more exposure. For example, if you would normally use an f/8 for a flash photograph, take three photographs, one each at f/8, F/5.6 and f/4. Another lighting issue involves lighting coverage—especially in large rooms. When using one electronic flash on the camera you will often have photographs with bright foregrounds and dark backgrounds. To increase lighting coverage you should consider using painting with light or multiple flash techniques. (These techniques are discussed in Chapter 2.)

Accurate exposure is necessary to record the subtle detail of burn patterns.

Fire scene photographs are often underexposed since charred walls tend to absorb, instead of reflect, light.

Photograph the interior of the building in a logical sequence. Consider photographing from areas of least damage to areas of most damage. When doing so, photograph all rooms and areas inside the building. As you photograph the interior of the structure, be sure to take overview photographs of each room to show the furniture and other contents of the room. If all the televisions, electronics, and computers are missing from the inside of an upscale home, the fire could have been set by the owner for insurance purposes or by burglars to conceal a crime.

Burn patterns at doorways indicate the spread of fire between rooms.

Burn patterns often show the direction of the spread of the fire.

As you move through the scene, photograph walls, ceilings, doorways and both sides of interior doors to show the direction of the spread of the fire. It is also important to photograph burn patterns within the scene. If you have not received training in arson investigation, it will be helpful to have an arson investigator direct you in what to photograph. Orientation in burn pattern photographs is critical. Placing arrows in photographs to indicate north and showing camera locations on sketches can be helpful when documenting burn patterns.

Furnaces should be photographed to show their condition and location relative to the origin of the fire. Electrical outlets, electrical extension cords and appliances should be examined and photographed if they could be related to the origin of the fire. Interior fire detection and suppression devices, such as smoke detectors, fire extinguishers and fire sprinkler systems, should be photographed.

Floors should be photographed to show the presence of accelerants.

Floors should be photographed to show the presence of accelerants. Any evidence of an incendiary device must be photographed. The area of the fire origin should be photographed thoroughly, before any excavation, showing the floor, ceiling, and nearby walls.

"V" patterns can indicate the origin of the fire.

During the investigation, the fire scene debris will be searched for evidence. This excavation process is carried out like an archeological dig, one level at a time. Any evidence found during this excavation process must be photographed.

Fire victims must be photographed. If a body is found in the structure it should be photographed in a manner similar to a homicide. Surviving victims should also be photographed to show the extent of their injuries. (Homicide and injury photography is discussed in Chapter 4.)

Vehicles

Vehicle fires should be photographed at the fire scene whenever possible. The area surrounding the vehicle should also be examined for evidence. Photograph any evidence located near the vehicle including footwear and tire impressions, and empty gasoline cans. If the vehicle has been taken to a wrecking yard, then the original scene should be examined for evidence and photographed.

Vehicle arson photographs include exterior views of the vehicle.

These three photographs clearly indicate that the origin of the fire was the front passenger seat. Note the broken windshield, heat damaged roof and "V" pattern on the interior of the passenger door.

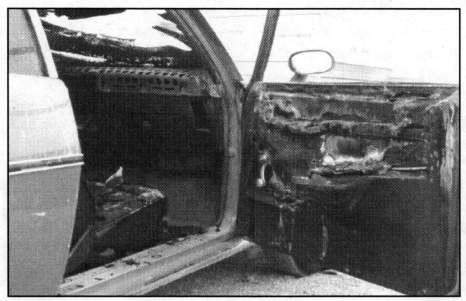

This interior view of the vehicle shows a burn pattern on the door that indicates the fire origin.

Documentation of a burned vehicle should begin with photographs of all four sides of vehicle. Next, photograph all four sides of vehicle with the hood, trunk and all doors standing open. Door hinges and window glass must be photographed to show the position of doors and windows at the time of the fire. Photograph the engine compartment, trunk, and passenger compartment. Be sure to include photographs of electrical wiring or anything else that may have been the origin of the fire. Photograph evidence of forced entry or vehicle theft.

EXPLOSION SCENES

Explosion scenes can be either the result of a criminal act or an accident. Before approaching an explosion scene, be certain the area is safe. Undetonated explosives may be present. In the case of criminal acts, suspects have been known to plant secondary devices designed to explode when police or fire personnel are at the scene. A meticulous search by a bomb squad should be conducted before a crime scene investigation begins. If the explosion involves a structure, do not enter the structure until you are sure the structure is safe and will not collapse.

The explosion scene must be thoroughly photographed. The scene area should be photographed with a series of photographs by beginning from the outside of the scene and working in toward the origin of the explosion. The origin is usually the area with most damage and will sometimes include a crater. Photograph any evidence associated with the explosion including pieces of clock mechanisms, wire and pipe.

The following photographs were taken at an explosion crime scene. A college student was constructing a homemade explosive device in his dormitory room. As the student mixed explosive materials in a small trash can, the materials exploded.

Exterior view shows the broken windows in the college campus dormitory room where the explosion occurred.

Interior view of room where the explosion occurred.

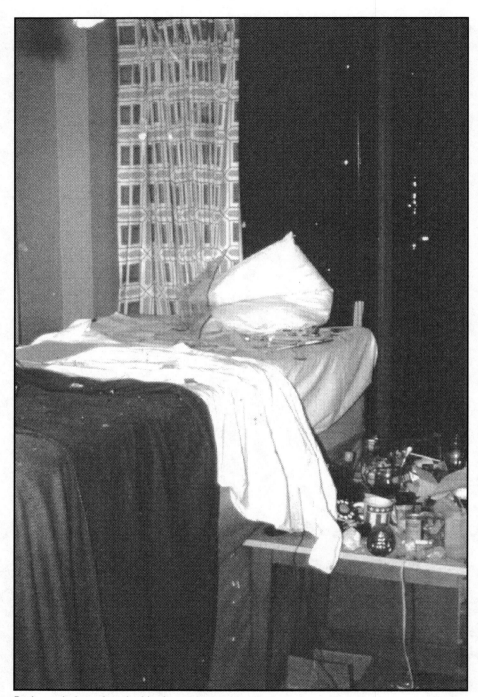

Broken window glass inside the scene.

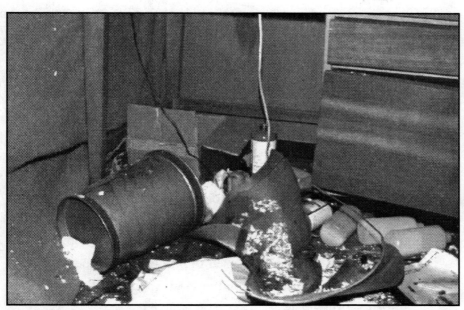

This view of the point of origin also shows the materials used to construct the explosive device.

This photograph shows a finger blown off the suspect's hand during the explosion.

SUMMARY

One goal in documenting a scene is to tell the story of what occurred through photography. Each crime scene has unique characteristics. With a little experience the crime scene photographer will learn what photographs should be taken at various scenes.

DISCUSSION QUESTIONS

1. How is black-and-white film more useful in some instances than color film?

2. What types of evidence should be photographed with black-and-white film?

3. What photographs can you take to identify the location of a residence or commercial building in a burglary investigation?

4. If the overview photographs do not show the location of a specific item of evidence, what should the photographer do?

5. What two steps should be used to photograph evidence?

6. How would you photograph the view a victim or witness had during a robbery?

7. What safety issues should you consider when photographing a fire scene?

8. Should black-and-white film or color film be use for fire and arson photography? Why?

9. What techniques should you consider to insure adequate lighting inside a dark fire scene?

10. What photographs are usually taken to document a vehicle fire?

EXERCISES AND ACTIVITIES

1. Photograph a residence as if burglarized.

ADDITIONAL RESOURCES

Almirall, Jose R., Furton, Kenneth G., (2004) *Analysis and Interpretation of Fire Scene Evidence*, CRC Press, Boca Raton, Florida 33431

Byrd, Mike, (2001) *Crime Scene Evidence: A Guide to the Recovery and Collection of Physical Evidence*, Staggs Publishing, Wildomar, California 92595

Duckworth, John E., (1983) *Forensic Photography*, Charles C. Thomas, Springfield, Illinois 62717

Fisher, Barry A. J., (2003) *Techniques of Crime Scene Investigation*, Seventh Edition, CRC Press, Boca Raton, Florida 33431

Miller, Larry S., (1998) *Police Photography*, Fourth Edition, Anderson Publishing Co., Cincinnati, Ohio 45202

National Fire Protection Association, Inc., (2001) *Guide for Fire and Arson Investigations*, NFPA, Quincy, Massachusetts 02269

Staggs, Steven, (2005) *Crime Scene and Evidence Photographer's Guide*, Second Edition, Staggs Publishing, Wildomar, California 92595

Chapter 6

Vehicles

OVERVIEW

A vehicle is often a part of a crime scene. A vehicle can be burglarized, vandalized, stolen, or used in the commission of a crime. Vehicles are also the primary subjects in traffic collision scenes. During these types of investigations the vehicles, and the evidence related to them, must be thoroughly photographed.

OBJECTIVES

At the end of this chapter, you will understand the use of photography in the processing of scenes that involve vehicles including:

1. Photographing a vehicle burglary scene
2. Photographing traffic collision scenes
3. Taking technical photographs of collision damage

BURGLARY TO VEHICLES

When called upon to photograph a vehicle burglary, normally you will have only one chance to photograph the vehicle and its associated evidence. Once the crime scene investigation, including the photography and collection of evidence, is completed, the control of the vehicle is usually given back to the owner. Therefore, it is important that you get all the photographs needed for documenting the case, and get them done properly, on the first attempt.

The first step in photographing a vehicle burglary is to photographically identify the vehicle. This can be done by photographing the vehicle identification number (VIN) and the license plate.

The VIN is normally on a metal plate found on the driver's side of the dashboard and is viewed through the windshield. When photographing a VIN plate you will need to fill the frame of the camera's viewfinder with the VIN plate, so you will need to use a macro lens or close-up accessory to position the camera about six inches from the plate. Also, since depth-of-field is shallow in close-up photographs, you must position the camera with the film plane parallel with the VIN plate so all the letters and numbers will be in sharp focus.

VIN plate photographed through a windshield.

Many times the VIN is easy to see and can be photographed without difficulty. If you can see the VIN clearly in your camera's viewfinder, and can read the letters and numbers on the plate, then no additional special photographic techniques are necessary. Just take the photograph.

However, if you cannot read the letters and numbers on the plate as you look through your camera's viewfinder, then one of two factors is likely interfering with your view. One possible factor is glare or reflection on the windshield that obscures your view. You might even see your own reflection from the windshield in the camera's viewfinder. To eliminate all, or part, of the glare and reflection from glass, you must use a polarizing filter over the camera's lens. As you position the polarizing filter on the lens you will see the glare and reflection lessen.

The other factor that could be interfering with your view is inadequate lighting. To improve lighting you can position a flashlight inside the vehicle on the dash to shine its light across the VIN plate. This works especially well on VIN plates with embossed or stamped letters and numbers; the oblique lighting creates shadows that make the letters and numbers more visible. You can then take a photograph with the illumination provided by the flashlight, or you can place an electronic flash in its place for the photograph. If you use an electronic flash be sure to position the flash far enough away from the VIN plate to avoid washing out the letters and numbers with too much light.

An additional problem that may present itself when photographing a VIN plate through a windshield is focusing with an auto–focus lens. Some auto-focus lenses have difficulty focusing accurately through glass. If this happens, switch off the auto-focus and manually focus the lens.

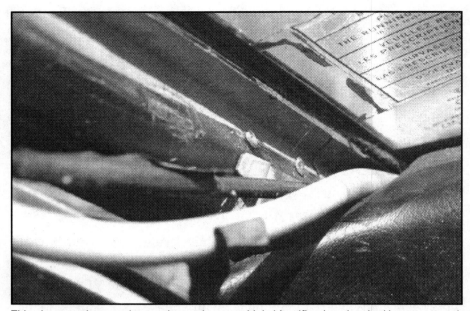

This photograph was taken to show where a vehicle identification plate had been removed. The rivets that held the VIN plate remain.

In addition to the VIN plate, there are identifying numbers and stickers in other locations on a vehicle. Some are hidden while others are easy to locate. A VIN sticker is usually located on the driver's side door or doorframe. If license plates or the VIN plate on the dash are missing or appear to have been switched or altered, the additional stickers and numbers should be photographed. An auto theft investigator or department of motor vehicles investigator may have to be consulted for the photographer to learn the location of hidden vehicle numbers. Use the same techniques discussed above when photographing VIN stickers and hidden numbers.

Vehicle license plates are photographed close enough to show detail of the registration renewal sticker.

The vehicle's license plate should also be photographed to identify the vehicle. When photographing a license plate you will need to fill the frame of the camera's viewfinder with the license plate. This should be done so the numbers on any registration renewal stickers are visible in the photograph. Reflectorized license plates can be a problem to photograph with an electronic flash. If the electronic flash is positioned on the camera and is pointing directly toward the license plate, the light will reflect back into the camera's lens, obscuring the letters and numbers. If you must use an electronic flash (e.g., a vehicle photographed at night) take the electronic flash off of the camera and position the flash at about a 45-degree angle to provide oblique lighting.

The second step in photographing a vehicle burglary is to photographically identify the location of the vehicle. This is done with overview photographs, which include a landmark, such as a street sign or building address. If the vehicle is in a location without distinctive landmarks (e.g., on a dirt road in the desert), the references to the vehicle's location in the investigator's report will have to do. In some cases investigators will use a GPS device to pinpoint the location of a vehicle.

The third step is to photograph all four sides of the vehicle. This will show the overall condition of the vehicle, such as broken windows, points of forced entry to the vehicle and the presence and absence of other damage caused by the burglars. Filling the frame of the camera's viewfinder with the side of the vehicle in order to show as much detail as possible should make these photographs useful.

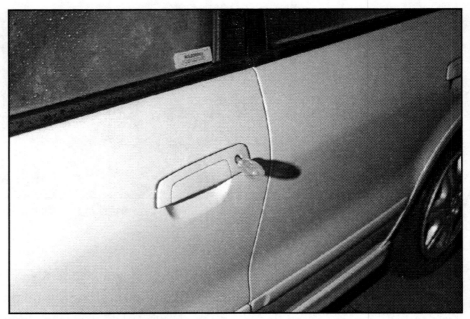

Point of entry on a vehicle burglary.

The next step is to photograph the point of entry to show as much detail as possible. A mid-range photograph will show the location of the point of entry on the vehicle and close-up photographs will show the detail of the point of entry. Evidence such as broken glass, pry marks and damaged locks are photographed. If anything you photograph can later be used to compare with a tool, such as pry marks, then a scale must be used on the same plane as the evidence in the photograph while positioning the camera so the film plane is parallel with the pry mark surface. (More information on positioning the camera and scale for this type of photography is detailed in Chapter 7, Evidence-Basic Concepts.)

Photographs of the interior of the vehicle show the condition of the interior and the presence of evidence.

The interior of the vehicle must also be photographed. These photographs will show the condition of the interior and the presence or absence of evidence. You will normally encounter deep shadows when photographing the interior of vehicles. If you expose the photographs of the interiors of vehicles using the daylight entering the vehicles through windows as your only light source, your photographs will usually include deep shadows that can conceal detail. It is best to use electronic flash whenever photographing the interior of a vehicle.

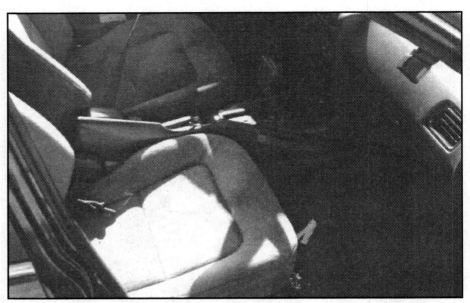

Photographing into a vehicle with existing light - exposures with strong sunlight entering a vehicle compartment usually results in photographs with deep shadows. Detail in the deep shadow areas may not be recorded on the film.

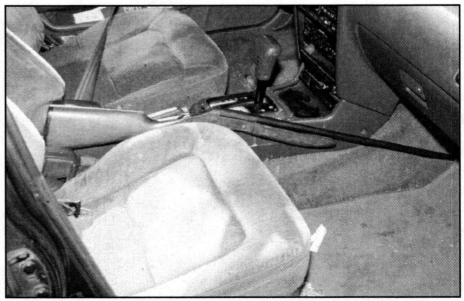

Photographing into a vehicle using electronic flash - detail in the deep shadow areas is recorded. Electronic flash is also useful for photographing into vehicle trunks and engine compartments.

Other evidence in and around the vehicle must be photographed. Evidence may include footwear impressions on the ground, damaged interiors, broken ignition switches, severed wires, tools left behind by the suspects, fingerprints before they are lifted, etc. Mid-range photographs will show the locations of the evidence and close-up photographs will show the detail of the evidence. If you photograph a footwear impression or tool mark that later might be used to compare with a suspect's shoe or tool, then a scale must be used in the photograph on the same plane as the evidence while positioning the camera so the film plane is parallel with the evidence. (More information on positioning the camera and scale for this type of photography is detailed in Chapter 7, Evidence-Basic Concepts.)

OTHER CRIME SCENES INVOLVING VEHICLES

Most of the steps and techniques described for photographing vehicle burglaries will also apply to other crimes involving vehicles, such as sexual assaults, arson, vandalism, and recovered stolen vehicles.

Collision Involving Vehicles

Traffic collision photographs should be taken as soon as possible. Every minute that passes increases the chance that important evidence can be altered or destroyed. Normally, you will have only one chance to photograph the scene, vehicles and associated evidence in a vehicle collision. Once the vehicle collision investigation (including the photography and collection of evidence) is completed, the control of the vehicle is usually given back to the owner or it is towed to a vehicle storage yard for safe keeping. Therefore, it is important that you get all the photographs needed for documenting the case on the first attempt.

Investigators photographing a traffic collision scene.

In all traffic collision investigations a diagram is drawn to document the roadway, marks on the roadway, final resting place of vehicles, etc. It may be helpful for other investigators who review your photographs to understand them if you indicate some of your camera locations on the diagram. Another technique would be to draw a separate field sketch that only shows the camera locations. This is most valuable to help orient the viewer for overview photographs, photographs of view obstructions and photographs taken to show drivers' points of view.

When photographing a collision scene, it is best to start from the outside edges of the scene and work toward the center. However, if the scene has not been stabilized and you are ready to begin photography, you may want to first photograph those things that may be changing. Examples include vehicles before they are cut apart in an attempt to remove injured occupants and vehicles before they are moved to open lanes to allow traffic to flow.

Use photographs to show the relationship of each vehicle with each other. If possible, include some permanent, recognizable landmark, such as a street sign, in some of the views to help orient the photographs. In some cases, such as multiple vehicle or fatal collisions, it may be helpful to show the overall scene with aerial photography.

Photograph debris or marks on the roadway, such as broken glass and gouges in the road surface. Photograph scrub marks on curbs, and damage to guardrails, utility poles and trees.

Photograph debris and marks on the roadway.

Photograph tire marks on roadway surfaces. Take one photograph from the direction of the mark to show the direction the vehicle was traveling. Take another photograph from the side to show the length of the tire mark. For long tire marks you may need to take a series of overlapping photographs, beginning at the location the mark began, and finishing where the mark ends. Photograph for the greatest depth-of-field possible. Often, the angle of the sun causes a glare or reflection on roadway surfaces and obscures clear views of tire marks. To eliminate all or part of the glare and reflection from the roadway surface you must use a polarizing filter over the camera's lens. As you position the polarizing filter on the lens you will see the glare and reflection lessen. Photograph the contact patch on the tire and the top of the tire mark to show tire tread type.

It is also important to show, with photographs, the view each driver had approaching the key point of the accident. This will show any view obstructions the driver may have had (e.g., fog, crests of hills, parked vehicles, overgrown vegetation), missing or damaged traffic control devices, etc. You can take these photographs either by taking the photographs from inside a similar vehicle at different points leading up to the point of impact, or by placing your camera on a tripod at the driver's eye level and taking a series of photographs leading up to the collision point. A 35mm lens, or a zoom lens set at 35mm, will provide a good representation of a person's view.

Photograph view obstructions and defective traffic control devices, such as this defective stop sign.

If there are witnesses to the collision, consider photographing the view from the point each witness observed the accident, at their eye level. Again, a 35mm lens, or a zoom lens set at 35mm, will provide a good representation of a person's view.

Photograph anything in the interior that indicates body contact, such as the hair and blood in this broken windshield.

When photographing an injury or fatal collision, be sure to photograph the vehicle's interior. Show anything in the interior that indicates body contact. In the case of fatal collisions where the body is still inside the vehicle, photograph the body from all available angles. Be sure to use an electronic flash when photographing the interiors of vehicles.

Hit and Run Collision Scenes

When photographing a hit and run collision scene you must photograph any evidence that may identify the hit and run vehicle. Photograph paint transfer, height of damage, pieces of suspect vehicle left at scene, tire impressions, and blood.

A vehicle struck from the rear received minor damage. An imprint in the dust on the rear bumper shows the other vehicle's license number. The dust imprint was photographed at the scene with diffused side lighting.

Photographing Collision Scenes at Night

Photographing traffic collision scenes at night can be difficult if you attempt to do so with electronic flash. Most electronic flash units will not provide adequate lighting for large areas at night. Typically, foregrounds in flash photographs will be bright and the backgrounds will be dark.

It is best to use either multiple flash, painting with light, or available light techniques for nighttime traffic collision scenes. These techniques can evenly light large scenes, extra-long tire marks, and the position of vehicles, which are some distance apart.

Painting with light — This large scene was photographed at night using "painting with light" to provide even lighting throughout the view. Photograph courtesy of the Huntington Beach (CA) Police Department.

Available light — This scene was photographed at night utilizing the ambient light provided by streetlights.

Technical Photographs of Damage to a Vehicle

Vehicle damage is photographed to help reconstruct the collision. An expert in collision reconstruction can use photographs to determine how one vehicle fitted against another vehicle or fixed object, from what direction the major force came, whether the vehicle rolled over, whether it had more than one collision during the accident, etc. These determinations can help prove or disprove a driver's statements. It is best to take vehicle damage photographs at the scene before the vehicles are moved so they will show no additional damage due to removal operations.

The first photograph should be taken to identify the vehicle. Photograph the vehicle identification number (VIN) either on the VIN plate or VIN sticker, and the license plate.

Next, photographs of the exterior of the vehicle are taken. Begin with the "basic eight" photographs of the vehicle. These include one photograph of the front of the vehicle, the rear, both sides, and a 45-degree angle shot of each corner of the vehicle. The "basic eight" photographs will show what areas are damaged as well as undamaged areas.

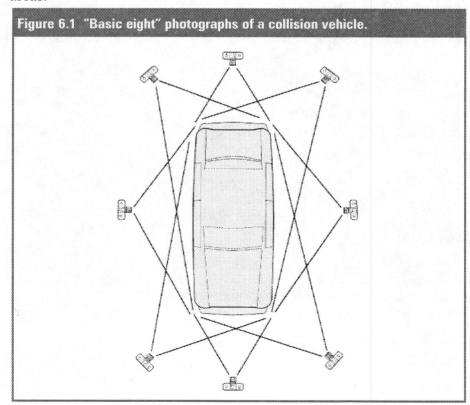

Figure 6.1 "Basic eight" photographs of a collision vehicle.

Next, more detailed photographs are taken of exterior damage. It is important to eliminate deep shadows in photographs of damage. Shadows will conceal detail that must be seen to do an adequate reconstruction of the collision. The best way to eliminate deep shadows is to use an electronic flash when photographing damage. When using an electronic flash, be aware that a flash mounted directly on the camera can cause reflections off of surfaces including metal, plastic, and glass. For many damage photographs it will be necessary to take the flash off of the camera and position the flash to provide oblique lighting.

Collision damage photographed with normal lighting. Shadows conceal the extent of the damage.

Collision damage photographed with electronic flash. Shadows are filled in with lighting to reveal the extent of the damage.

When photographing details of collision damage, it is important to take at least two photographs of each damage area. The first photograph shows where on the vehicle the damage is located and the second photograph shows the detail of the damage. The first is necessary since a close-up photograph of damage may not indicate where the damage is located on the vehicle. For example, damage on a door may look the same whether it is the left or right door. All close-up photographs of damage must include a scale. Use a scale with markings and numbers large enough to be seen clearly in the photograph. Position scales on the same plane as the damage to show height from the ground and the size of the damage.

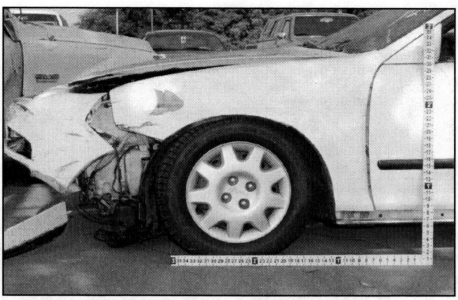

When photographing collision damage, use an electronic flash to fill in shadows and scales with large, easy to read numbers.

Photographs of the vehicle roof should also be taken. This may show the amount of crush, principal direction of force and, in cases of rollover, the direction the vehicle rolled. While it is best to photograph the roof from directly overhead, keeping the camera's film plane parallel with the roof, you may have to settle for photographing at different angles while standing on a ladder.

Many times it is important to view damage to the undercarriage of the vehicle. If the vehicle is going to be towed you can ask the two truck operator to lift one end of the vehicle as high as possible so you can photograph the undercarriage.

Damage to wheels and tires should be photographed. This may reveal the condition of the tire prior to the collision (e.g., amount of tread on the tire, uneven wear from misalignment, improper inflation) and damage to the tire or wheel (e.g., blow out or dents in the rim). When photographing the tread on a tire you may need to use oblique lighting to best show wear-patterns, depth-of-tread, and defects.

This photograph of the tread on a tire was photographed with oblique lighting.

Since modifications to vehicles can change the vehicle's performance characteristics, and possibly contribute to the cause of the collision, be sure to photograph any modifications to the vehicle. This includes tinted windows that may have obscured a driver's vision.

Any other damage or conditions of interest on the exterior of the vehicle should be photographed. This might include the filaments of light bulbs to determine if the light was on at the time of breakage, paint transfer from other vehicles, and damage that appears to have occurred in a previous collision.

Next, the vehicle's interior should be photographed. Photograph bloodstains and any areas where it appears the occupants' bodies came into contact with interior surfaces of the vehicle. Photograph the condition of seat belts and air bags that have deployed during the collision. Photograph the condition of the seats, child restraint systems, steering wheel and rearview mirror. Complete your photographs of the interior by including any damage or conditions of interest.

The filament in a broken lamp can best be photographed in a laboratory setting.

Some items of evidence will be collected and can be photographed in more detail in the crime laboratory. For example, the filament in a broken lamp can best be photographed in a laboratory setting. A piece of broken headlight glass found at the scene of a hit-and-run collision can be matched with the broken headlight on a suspect vehicle. (More information on this type of evidence photography is detailed in Chapter 9, Evidence Photography In the Laboratory.)

SUMMARY

Vehicles, whether involved in property crimes, crimes against persons, or traffic collisions, can provide a great deal of evidence for investigations. When the crime scene photographer carefully and completely photographs vehicles and their related evidence the investigation will benefit with valuable documentation that can be used by investigators and, ultimately, a court or jury to understand exactly how evidence appeared at the time of the incident.

DISCUSSION QUESTIONS

1. Why is it so important to get all the photographs needed for documenting a vehicle burglary case on the first attempt?

2. How do you photographically identify a vehicle?

3. What can be done to improve photographs involving reflection off windshields or glare off roadways?

4. How should you photograph a reflectorized license plate with an electronic flash?

5. Why is it best to use an electronic flash whenever photographing the interior of a vehicle?

6. What can be shown by photographing the view of each driver as they approached the key point of the collision?

7. How would you photograph the view a driver had just prior to a collision?

8. What focal length lens will provide a good representation of a person's view?

9. What techniques can be used for photographing large collision scenes at night?

10. Describe the steps and technique for photographing collision damage to the right front corner of a vehicle.

EXERCISES AND ACTIVITIES

1. Photo the VIN of a vehicle.

2. Set up a short daytime scene in your driveway or parking lot. Photograph the roadway, car (pretend it is damaged or mark a damaged area with tape) and the interior of the car.

3. Set up a short nighttime scene in your driveway or parking lot. Photograph the roadway, car (pretend it is damaged or mark a damaged area with tape) and the interior of the car.

ADDITIONAL RESOURCES

Fricke, Lynn and Baker, J., (1985) *Photography for Traffic-Accident Investigation*, Northwestern University Traffic Institute, Evanston, Illinois 60204

Baker, Kenneth S., (2002) *Traffic Collision Investigation*, Northwestern University Traffic Institute, Evanston, Illinois 60204

Murray, Jack, (1997) *Photographing Vehicles for Litigation*, Institute of Police Technology and Management, University of North Florida, Jacksonville, Florida 32224

Rivers, R. W., (1992) *Traffic Accident Investigator's Manual*, Second Edition, Charles C. Thomas Publisher, Springfield, Illinois 62704

Staggs, Steven, (2005) *Crime Scene and Evidence Photographer's Guide*, Second Edition, Staggs Publishing, Wildomar, California 92595

Chapter 7

Evidence - Basic Concepts

CHAPTER OVERVIEW

It is possible to reconstruct a crime by analyzing the location and appearance of physical evidence found at the crime scene. Therefore, the location and appearance of evidence must be accurately documented. Photographs, supported with notes and crime scene diagrams, help investigators, and ultimately a jury, to understand the evidence and its importance to the case.

All evidence located at the crime scene must be documented photographically before it is collected. These photographs of evidence are done after the overview photographs have been taken of the scene. After evidence has been collected, it may be necessary to take more detailed photographs of some of the items of evidence in a laboratory setting where specialized photographic techniques may be employed.

CHAPTER OBJECTIVES

At the end of this chapter you will be able to use the general principles of evidence photography including:
1. The number of photographs to take of items of evidence
2. Using scales and marking devices
3. Camera and scale orientation
4. Lighting
5. Exposure
6. Focusing
7. Establishing the location of evidence with a series of photographs

GENERAL PRINCIPLES IN EVIDENCE PHOTOGRAPHY

First, we need to be aware of the general principles for documenting evidence with photography. These general principles involve the number of photographs to be taken, the use of scales and marking devices, camera orientation, lighting, and focusing.

Number of Photographs

When photographing most evidence at the crime scene you must take at least two photographs of each item of evidence. There can be some exceptions, such as in photographing fingerprints (which will be discussed in the next chapter), but normally two photographs of each item of evidence are needed.

The first photograph should be a mid-range view of the item of evidence to show its location in the scene and how the item is related to its surroundings. This photograph must show clearly where an item is located in relation to other parts of the immediate area of the scene. The immediate area of the scene will also be shown in your series of overview photographs of the larger area of the scene. For example, an overview photograph shows the area of a room, which contained a sofa, coffee table and the body of a victim. The mid-range photograph would show the body and a knife alongside the body, and in this case a mid-range photograph shows where the evidence, in this example a knife, is located in the scene.

If you happen to have several items of evidence that are located close to each other, you may be able to show all the items of evidence in one mid-range photograph. Again, the purpose of this first photograph is to show where individual items of evidence are located within the crime scene.

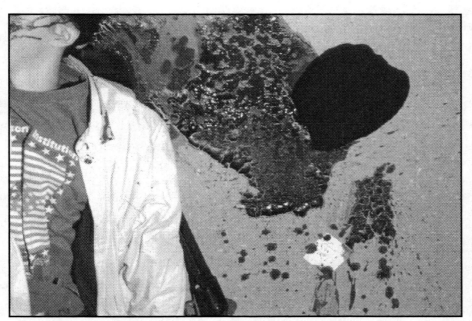

A mid-range view of the item of evidence shows its location in the scene and how the item is related to its surroundings.

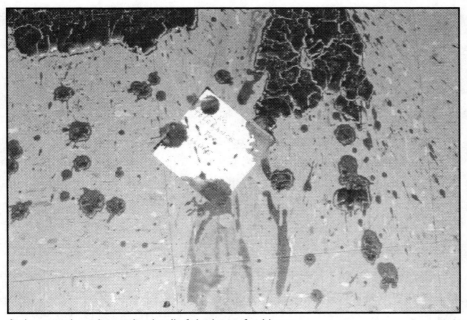

A close-up view shows the detail of the item of evidence.

The second photograph of the item of evidence should be a close-up view to bring out the detail of the object itself. The item of evidence is photographed without moving the evidence or anything surrounding it that may also appear in the photograph.

In some situations, something may have to be moved in order to photograph evidence. In such a situation it is best to photograph everything else in that area of the scene first, and then photograph the area that must be disturbed as each modification is made. For example, if you need to photograph items of evidence under a victim's body you would first photograph the area around the body, the body from different angles, and then after the body is moved by the coroner or investigators, photograph the additional evidence.

Often, additional photographs of items of evidence must be taken following the two photographs just discussed. These additional photographs may be needed to show more detail in the evidence. They can sometimes be taken without moving the evidence or may need to be taken after collecting the evidence. Also, these additional photographs may be needed to show different sides or surfaces of the evidence that were not visible where the evidence was originally located, or may require specialized lighting or techniques, such as macro photography or ultraviolet photography. These photographs may be taken at the scene, perhaps on the top of a portable table at the command post, or later at the crime laboratory.

Using Scales and Marking Devices

Frequently scales are used in photographs of evidence. However, not every item of evidence documented photographically at a crime scene requires a scale in the photograph. For example, a photograph of a gun on the floor at a homicide scene usually does not need a scale. The gun will be collected as evidence and will not change its dimensions. It can be measured at any time if its size later becomes an issue. Scales should only be used when necessary to show relative size in a photograph or when the photograph will be used to later make a comparison, such as a comparison between the photograph of a footwear impression from the scene and a suspect's shoe. It should be noted however, that some departments require by policy, that a scale appear in every photograph of evidence.

First, photograph the item of evidence without any scale or marking device.

Second, photograph the item of evidence with the scale or marking device.

Marking devices (such as numbers, arrows and identification cards) should only be used in photographs when necessary. Numbering devices for each item of evidence are unnecessary unless similar items appear in the scene. For example, when there are several footwear impressions at a scene, each impression should be photographed with a numbering device to clearly differentiate one from another and to indicate where each was located within the crime scene. However, some departments require by policy, that a numbering device appear in every photograph of evidence.

Other devices, such as pointers or arrows, are sometimes used in evidence photographs to point out an item that may be hard to see or to indicate north. For example, a bullet fragment mixed in with broken glass may be difficult to see so a pointer or an arrow may be used to show its location. An arrow may be used in a photograph of a footwear impression to orient the evidence and indicate a suspect's direction of travel.

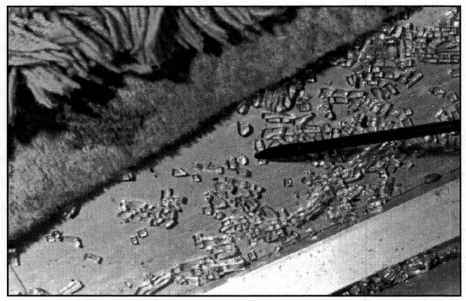

A pointer was used in this photograph to show the location of a bullet fragment mixed in with broken glass.

When a scale or marking device is used in a photograph, two photographs must be taken. The first photograph should not contain a scale or marking device. This is done so the area that will be blocked or covered with the scale or marking device in the second photograph can be clearly seen in the first photograph. The second photograph would then contain the scale or marking device. This two-photograph technique is done so that there is one photograph that shows the area without anything introduced into it by the investigator. Then it cannot be argued that there are no photographs of the scene before it was altered by placing scales or marking devices in it, or that the scale or marking device in a photograph was concealing other evidence.

Always use a measuring or marking device that cannot be mistaken for evidence. Sometimes an investigator will be without a scale and will place a business card, writing pen, or other item in a photograph to show scale. Using anything other than a scale in the photograph is confusing. Such items may be mistaken for evidence. Always be sure you have a sufficient supply of scales in your identification kit.

Camera and Scale Orientation for Close-up Photographs

When taking close-up photographs to show the detail of the evidence, you should whenever possible, position your camera to minimize distortion in the photograph. This can be accomplished by keeping the camera's film plane parallel with the plane of the evidence. In other words, position the camera at a 90-degree angle to the evidence. Taking a photograph with the camera positioned at an oblique angle will introduce distortion into the photograph. This becomes extremely important when photographing evidence in which the photograph will be used for measurements such as bloodstain evidence, or comparison purposes, such as footwear impression evidence.

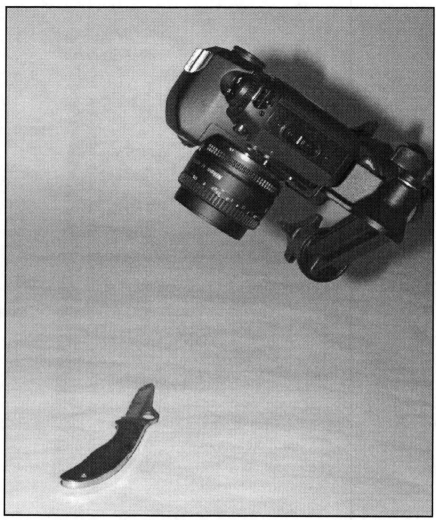

Improper camera position for photographing evidence. The camera is positioned at an oblique angle to the evidence.

Proper camera position for photographing evidence. The camera's film plane is parallel with the evidence.

When a scale is used in a photograph the scale must be positioned on the same plane as the evidence. Taking a photograph with the scale on a different plane will introduce distortion into the photograph and the scale will be virtually useless. This also becomes extremely important when photographing evidence in which the photograph will be used for measurements, such as bloodstain evidence, or comparison purposes, such as footwear impression evidence.

Improper scale position for photographing evidence. The scale is not positioned on the same plane as the evidence.

Proper scale position for photographing evidence. The scale is positioned on the same plane as the evidence.

Lighting

One of the most important skills for a crime scene photographer to master is the proper use of light. If you always rely on existing light or direct flash to light your evidence, you will have many poor photographs. Understanding and using proper lighting techniques will result in high-quality photographs. Each time you prepare to photograph an item of evidence, stop and analyze the lighting you are using. You may find that by changing the direction or intensity of the light on the evidence, or by taking several photographs with the lighting from different angles, you will have improved results.

When evaluating lighting, remember what you see in the viewfinder is what you will get in your photograph. Position the camera and examine the image in the viewfinder. If the existing (ambient) lighting provides adequate results you may be able to take the photograph with the existing light.

If existing lighting does not provide the desired results you must change the lighting. You can preview how the photograph will look with other light angles by moving a lighting source, such as a flashlight, around to different angles while looking in the camera's viewfinder. When the best angle of light for the evidence is observed, place the electronic flash, or other light source, in that position for the photograph.

A wide-angle diffuser or handkerchief over the flash head will soften the light from an electronic flash.

When using an electronic flash, beware of overexposure from too much flash. For close-up photography you can reduce the intensity of the flash by using wide-angle diffuser, handkerchief or other diffusion material placed over the electronic flash head, or by positioning the flash further away from the subject. This will help avoid overexposure.

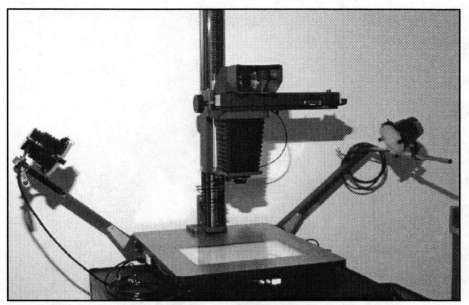

A laboratory copy stand is most efficient in photographing evidence in a controlled setting.

A portable copy stand or a tripod can be set up at the crime scene to photograph evidence.

Other lighting devices may be effective for certain types of evidence. They include micro flash (two small electronic flash units on adjustable arms) and ring light flash units.

Ring Light Electronic Flash

Ring light flash units are best in lighting non-reflective evidence such as injuries on a victim. A ring light flash provides shadow-free lighting and low contrast. A ring light flash is usually not suitable for photographing textured items or impressions, such as tool marks and footwear impressions, because it eliminates the shadows that help to show detail in such evidence.

Film

Mid-range photographs, which show the location of evidence, are normally taken with color film. The use of color film provides photographs that look natural and are easier to understand than black-and-white photographs. However, when doing close-up photographs of evidence the crime scene photographer must decide whether to use color or black-and-white film. Some evidence photographs may need to show the color of an item, such as the color of paint used in a vandalism case, or to identify evidence on a background, such as bloodstain on a multicolored wall. In these cases, color print film would be used.

Other types of evidence should be photographed with black-and-white film to show greater detail because black-and-white film provides more contrast than most color films. Fingerprints, impressions and tool marks are usually photographed with black-and-white film.

Exposure

Correct exposure is critical in evidence photography. Incorrect exposures can result in lost detail in a photograph. Most evidence photography is done with either ambient light, which may be steady burning lamps or simply the light existing at the location, or electronic flash.

Ambient light exposures can often be metered with the camera's internal exposure meter or an external exposure meter. However, before relying on any reflected light exposure meter, you should determine if the meter will be providing an accurate reading due to the subject or background about to be photographed. Exposure meters use 18 percent reflectance in determining exposure. If you are photographing evidence or a background that does not have 18 percent reflectance, then the exposure reading can be in error. For example, when the evidence you are photographing is a dusted fingerprint on a white surface, an exposure meter will, as always, base its exposure settings on 18 percent reflectance. Since the subject matter in the photograph is almost all white, the meter will provide exposure settings that result in an underexposed photograph. Much of the detail in the photograph will be lost. A second example would be a dark item, such as a section of charred wall at an arson scene. The exposure meter will base its settings on 18 percent reflectance and would provide exposure settings that result in an overexposed photograph. Much of the detail in the charred wall will be lost.

When using ambient light for evidence photographs you can ensure accurate exposures by using an 18 percent gray card. Position the 18 percent gray card in front of the exposure meter, or in front of the camera lens if you are using the camera's exposure meter, to obtain the correct exposure settings. Be sure the ambient light is falling on the 18 percent gray card the same as it is falling on your evidence. Use the settings indicated by the exposure meter for the photograph. In many cases, bracketing should also be considered. Bracketing will provide a series of photographs at different exposures. Later, the best exposures from the series of photographs can be used for the investigation.

Normal electronic flash exposures can be done in either automatic or manual flash when photographing evidence. Through-the-lens (TTL) electronic flash unit exposures will be controlled automatically by the camera's TTL flash metering system. When using electronic flash, bracketing should also be considered.

Focusing

When taking close-up photographs one of the most common problems encountered is shallow dept-of-field. Therefore, accurate focusing is critical. One important technique regarding focusing for close-up photography is to avoid focusing on the scale. Instead, be sure to focus on the evidence. While it is frequently easier to focus on the markings or edge of the scale, the scale may not always be on the exact plane of the evidence. It is better to have a sharp image of the evidence and a slightly out of focus scale than to have a sharp image of the scale and the evidence out of focus.

The best way to get sharp images is to stabilize the camera on a tripod or copy stand. Once the camera is stabilized, fine focusing can be done with greater accuracy. When the camera is stabilized you can use a combination of focusing with the lens and moving the camera and evidence closer together or further apart to get the sharpest focus.

If you are hand-holding the camera while taking a close-up it is usually difficult to get the sharpest focus. This is because if you are both moving the camera slightly and focusing you are in effect chasing a moving target. To focus close-up while hand-holding the camera you should first rough size (scale) the subject by focusing with the lens focusing ring. When you have the evidence just about focused in your viewfinder, stop focusing the lens with the focusing ring. Then you can fine focus the subject by moving the camera in and out from the subject. While maintaining the fine focus by moving the camera in and out slightly, lightly depress the shutter button to take the photograph.

ESTABLISHING THE LOCATION OF EVIDENCE WITH A SERIES OF PHOTOGRAPHS

Sometimes it may not be possible to show the location and detail of evidence with just two photographs, as discussed earlier in this chapter. Evidence may be located in an area with no landmarks nearby, such as in an open area of the desert. In this case, the use of a GPS device (to give location) and a compass (to indicate the direction in which the evidence is oriented) may be the only way to document the exact position of the evidence. In such a case you could record the GPS information in your notes and in the photograph of the evidence, include an arrow that is oriented to indicate north.

However, if the item of evidence is in a remote area but there is a landmark relatively near, you can show the location of the evidence with a series of photographs. Begin with an overview photograph that shows the general area. In this photograph include a recognizable landmark. Then take a series of photographs that lead the viewer to the location of the evidence.

The first photograph includes a recognizable landmark.

The second photograph points to the location of the evidence, in the example, toward the end of the street.

Subsequent photographs lead the viewer to the location of the evidence.

The last photograph shows the evidence at the exact location of the evidence.

CLOSE-UP LENSES AND DEVICES

Close-up equipment — clockwise from top left: bellows, macro lens, reversing ring, close-up filters.

To record fine detail when photographing evidence, the item of evidence should fill the frame of the camera's viewfinder. Since most normal lenses are designed to focus from about three feet to infinity, they cannot focus close enough to be effective when photographing small items of evidence. A standard lens can be used to photograph a footwear impression, but cannot be focused close enough to photograph a latent fingerprint. A macro lens or some type of close-up accessory will be needed when a close-up photograph requires the lens to focus closer than three feet.

A macro lens is a lens that is designed for moderate close-up focusing. True macro photography begins when the image size on the film equals the actual subject size (1:1 magnification) or is magnified to larger than life size. Not all macro lenses can actually produce a 1:1 image on the film. However, macro lenses that come close to 1:1 magnification can usually be used for photographing items of evidence as small as a latent fingerprint.

Close-up accessories can be used in place of a macro lens. Close-up accessories include 1:1 adapters, extension tubes, extension bellows, reversing rings, and close-up filters.

1:1 adapter screws onto the front of the camera's normal lens.

A 1:1 adapter is a device that screws onto the front of the camera's normal lens. The 1:1 adapter magnifies the image to produce a life-sized image on the film. 1:1 adapters can produce photographs with out-of-focus edges if you use large lens openings. To increase sharpness, use a lens opening of f/8 or smaller when photographing evidence with a 1:1 adapter.

Extension tubes are placed between the camera body and the lens to increase magnification.

Extension tubes and extension bellows extend the lens away from the film creating 1:1 or greater magnification.

Reverse-mounting the lens creates magnification.

A reversing ring allows you to reverse-mount a normal lens on the camera. This results in enough magnification to effectively photograph an item of evidence about the size of a latent fingerprint.

Close-up filters screw on the front of a normal lens to provide increased magnification.

Close-up filters are relatively inexpensive lenses that screw on the front of the camera's normal lens. These close-up filters are rated in diopters of magnifying power such as +1, +2 and +3. The close-up filters can be combined to make new powers (e.g., a +2 combined with a +3 becomes +5). When these close-up filters are attached to a normal lens the +1 focuses at about 20 inches, the +2 focuses at about 13 inches, the +3 focuses at about ten inches, and the +5 focuses at about four inches. When using more than one close-up filter on a camera lens, the filters should be placed on the lens in descending order. For example, when using a +1 and a +2 filter, place the +2 on the camera lens first, followed by the +1. Close-up filters can produce photographs with out-of-focus edges if you use large lens openings. To increase sharpness use a lens opening of f/8 or smaller when photographing evidence with close-up filters.

SUMMARY

In any crime scene investigation, the location and appearance of physical evidence must be documented. Photographs play a key role in this type of documentation. Understanding and using the basic concepts in this chapter will enable the crime scene photographer to take the high quality photographs necessary for successful investigations.

DISCUSSION QUESTIONS

1. At a minimum, how many photographs of each item of evidence are usually necessary?

2. Give an example of a photograph in which you would use an arrow or pointer.

3. Why is it necessary to take a photo without a scale or marking device before taking a photo with the scale or marking device when photographing evidence?

4. What could be a result of not taking a photo of evidence without a scale or marking device before taking a photo with a scale or marking device?

5. Why is it important to always be sure you have a sufficient supply of scales in your I.D. kit?

6. How should the camera and scale be positioned relative to an item of evidence?

7. How can you preview how the lighting will look in an evidence photo?

8. How can you help avoid over-exposure in close-up photo?

9. How is an 18 percent gray card used to get accurate ambient light photos?

10. What is a macro lens? What can be used in place of a macro lens?

EXERCISES AND ACTIVITIES

1. Set-up a simulated crime scene and take the following photographs: overview, mid-range, and close-up.

2. Using the same simulated crime scene, take one photograph with a scale and one without the scale in the scene.

3. Using an electronic flash, take one photograph without a "diffuser" and a second one using a "diffuser or handkerchief."

4. At a simulated crime scene, take the following pictures:
    *   Includes a recognizable landmark
    *   Points to the location of the evidence
    *   Leads the viewer to the evidence
    *   Depicts the exact location of the evidence

ADDITIONAL RESOURCES

Byrd, Mike, (2001) *Crime Scene Evidence: A Guide to the Recovery and Collection of Physical Evidence*, Staggs Publishing, Wildomar, California 92595

Duckworth, John E., (1983) *Forensic Photography*, Charles C. Thomas, Springfield, Illinois 62717

Fisher, Barry A. J., (2003) *Techniques of Crime Scene Investigation*, Seventh Edition, CRC Press, Boca Raton, Florida 33431

McDonald, James A., (1992) *Close-up and Macro Photography for Evidence Technicians*, Second Edition, Phototext Books, Palatine, Illinois 60067

Miller, Larry S., (1998) *Police Photography, Fourth Edition*, Anderson Publishing Co., Cincinnati, Ohio 45202

Staggs, Steven, (2005) *Crime Scene and Evidence Photographer's Guide*, Second Edition, Staggs Publishing, Wildomar, California 92595

Chapter 8

Evidence Photography At The Crime Scene

CHAPTER OVERVIEW

Several types of evidence are commonly found at crime scenes. Each item of evidence must be documented photographically, showing its location and appearance. In the previous chapter, the basic concepts of evidence photography were discussed. This chapter provides specialized techniques for photographing evidence commonly found at crime scenes.

CHAPTER OBJECTIVES

At the end of this chapter, you will be able to photograph several types of evidence commonly found at crime scenes including:

1. Impressions
2. Tool marks
3. Fingerprints
4. Bloodstain
5. Bullet paths

INTRODUCTION EVIDENCE AT THE CRIME SCENE

As you study this chapter, be aware that many of the techniques can also be applied in a laboratory setting. For example, fingerprints on an item that will be collected as evidence may be either photographed at the scene before packaging or later in the laboratory. Several factors may be considered in this example. It may be safer to photograph the fingerprint at the scene if there is a chance the fingerprint will be damaged when the evidence is transported to the laboratory, or it may be more effective to photograph the fingerprint in the laboratory due to the specialized lighting available on a copy stand. It will be up to the crime scene photographer to determine which would be the best course of action for each item of evidence.

IMPRESSIONS

Footwear and tire impressions are perhaps the most overlooked evidence at a crime scene. When impressions are collected, it is possible that identifications can be made linking a suspect or vehicle to the crime. Impression evidence can be collected by casting (filling the impression with a compound that hardens and retains the shape and characteristics of the impression) and with photography. Photographs of impressions are often used to make positive identifications, but casting of impressions provides the best evidence. This is because impressions are three-dimensional and casting preserves three-dimensional evidence. The depth of tread and imperfections on the sides of the tread are preserved with casting. At major crime scenes, impressions should be photographed before they are casted. Photography is done first because casting the impression will destroy the original impression and eliminate the ability to photograph the impression afterward. In addition, photographs of an impression are taken in case there is a problem with the cast. If the casting fails the photograph may be used to make an identification.

At minor crime scenes, impressions are usually photographed without casting. If the impression is properly photographed, positive identification linking a suspect or vehicle to the crime is possible.

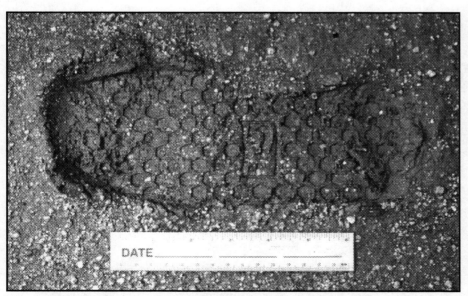

Take a photograph to establish the location of the impression within the crime scene. Follow with a close-up photograph of the impression.

When taking photographs of footwear or tire impressions, begin with a photograph to show where the impression is located in the crime scene. It is important to include a recognizable landmark in the photograph so the location of the impression is understood. If the impression is near a landmark, such as in a flowerbed at the corner of a house, a mid-range photograph probably would be adequate to show the location of the impression. If the impression is farther away from a recognizable landmark, such as an impression on a dirt driveway 20 yards from the house, additional photographs would be necessary. An overview photograph showing the driveway with the house in the background would be followed with a mid-range photograph of the impression on the driveway. It may be necessary to include an evidence marker in both the overview and mid-range photographs to clearly show the location of the impression in the photographs.

There may be times where it is not possible to show the exact location of an impression with photographs. The impression may be located in an area with no recognizable landmarks nearby, such as in an open area of the desert. In this case, the use of a GPS device (to give location) and a compass (to indicate the direction in which the evidence is oriented) may be the only way to document the exact position of the impression. In such a case, you could record the GPS information in your notes and in the photograph of the impression, include an arrow that is oriented to indicate north.

Photographing Impressions: Use a scale on the same plane as the impression. Keep the film plane parallel to the plane of the impression. Position the electronic flash or light source at angles that highlight the detail in the impression. Preview the photograph by using a strong light source at different angles.

After photographically documenting the location of the impression, you must take close-up photographs to show the detail of the impression. It is best to photograph impression evidence with black-and-white film. Black-and-white film provides more contrast and detail than most color films.

To take a close-up photograph of an impression, place the camera on a tripod and position the camera so the camera's film plane is parallel with the impression. This will minimize distortion in the photograph. An angle finder can be used to measure the angle of the impression and then, by placing the angle finder on the camera's eyepiece, the angle of the camera can be adjusted to match the angle of the impression. The film plane will then be parallel to the impression.

An angle finder can be used to position the camera so the film plane is parallel with the impression. Measure the angle of the impression and then adjust the camera to the same angle.

Next, place a scale alongside the impression. When photographing a footwear impression, use an "L" shaped scale. When photographing a tire impression use, a long straight scale alongside the impression. Place the scale approximately one inch away from the impression and on the same plane as the impression. If necessary, press the scale into the ground until it is the same depth as the impression.

Orientation of the impression is also important. The direction a footwear impression faces could be important to the investigation. For example, in a residential burglary it would be important to show that the footwear impressions in a flowerbed face the window that was used by the suspect to enter the residence. Showing the orientation can be accomplished with a mid-range photograph that includes the window and the impressions. If it is difficult to see the orientation of the impressions in the mid-range photograph, an arrow (indicating north) can be included in both the mid-range and close-up photographs.

In order to get as much detail recorded on the film as possible, your camera should be positioned so that the frame of your viewfinder is filled with the impression and scale.

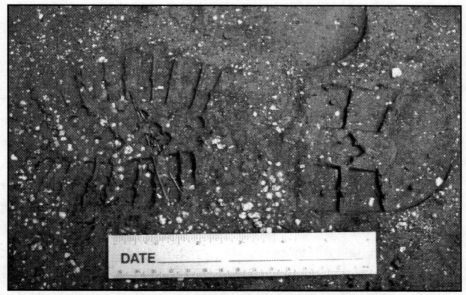

Place the scale approximately one inch away from the impression and on the same plane as the impression.

Most of the detail recorded in an impression photograph will be visible due to the small shadows that appear within the impression. The existing shadowing from daylight does not always provide the best results. The position of the sun may actually provide the least desirable results. If you settle for the lighting provided by the sun, you would usually have poor quality impression photographs. In fact, it is necessary to take several photographs of each impression, with the lighting from different angles, to show all the detail within an impression.

The most effective way to ensure you are using the best angles of lighting is "preview the photograph" by looking at lighting from several different angles. To do this, shade the impression with a large piece of cardboard. Then, position a strong light source, such as a powerful flashlight, at different angles to find the light angles that show the best detail in the impression. As you move the lighting, you will see the results you will get by looking into your viewfinder. Then position your electronic flash at the best angles for the photographs. You will usually need two people to help you with this technique, one to hold the cardboard, and the other to move the flashlight and position the electronic flash.

Another lighting technique would be to take a series of photographs with the electronic flash or light source at six different angles. Two photographs would be taken from each of three directions, one with the electronic flash positioned at a 25-degree angle and the other positioned at a 45-degree angle. You will probably want to use a lower angle for impressions in dust and for very shallow impressions, and a higher angle for deep impressions.

Impressions in snow are photographed with the same techniques detailed above. One additional issue with photographing impressions in the snow is exposure. Remember that the camera's metering system provides settings for normal lighting, which is 18 percent reflectance. Since the subject matter in the photograph is almost all white, the meter will provide exposure settings that result in an underexposed photograph. Much of the detail in the photograph will be lost. When using ambient light for photographs in the snow you can ensure accurate exposures by using an 18 percent gray card. Position the 18 percent gray card in front of the camera lens to obtain the correct exposure settings. Be sure the ambient light is falling on the 18 percent gray card the same as it is falling on your evidence. Use the settings indicated by the exposure meter for the photograph. In many cases, bracketing should also be considered. Bracketing will provide a series of photographs at different exposures. Later, the best exposures from the series of photographs can be used for the investigation. This applies to the overview, mid-range and close-up photographs of snow scenes and evidence.

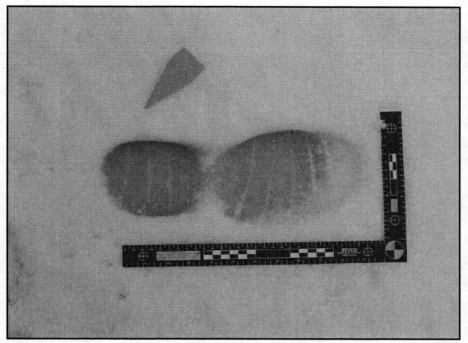

This photograph of a shoe impression in the snow was taken using electronic flash and the camera's TTL flash metering system. Since the snow is more reflective than normal subjects, the resulting photograph becomes underexposed.

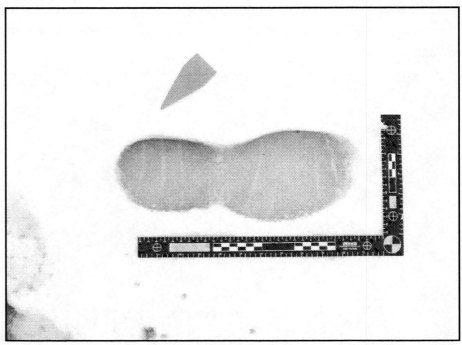

This photograph is better exposed after adjusting the camera's exposure compensation for two f/stops of increased exposure.

When using an electronic flash to photograph footwear impressions in the snow, it is likely your photographs will be underexposed. This is because the automatic and TTL electronic flash systems are designed to control the duration of the flash by reading the light reflected off normal subjects. Since the snow will reflect more light than a normal subject the automatic and TTL systems will usually shut off the flash before an adequate exposure is made. The resulting photographs can be underexposed by about two f/stops.

You can adjust your camera to gain back the two f/stops of exposure. When using an automatic camera adjust the camera's exposure control setting to a setting of +2. When using a manual camera close down the lens aperture by two f/stops (e.g., if a normal flash photograph requires a f/11, change the aperture to f/5.6). In many cases, bracketing should also be considered. Bracketing will provide a series of photographs at different exposures. Later, the best exposures from the series of photographs can be used for the investigation.

Photograph footwear impressions with a tripod, "L" shaped scale, and an arrow to indicate north.

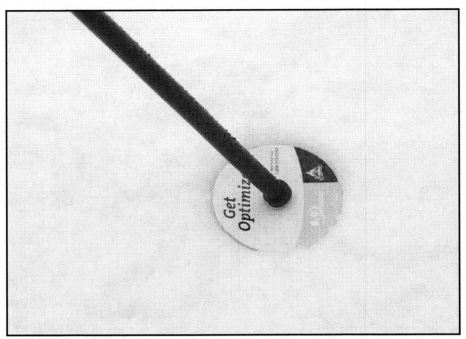

Place computer or audio compact discs under the tripod legs to stabilize the tripod in snow, mud or sand.

When working with a tripod in the snow it is sometimes difficult to steady the tripod when it tends to sink into the snow. Placing computer or audio compact discs under the tripod legs will help stabilize the tripod. This same technique works when using tripods on mud or sand.

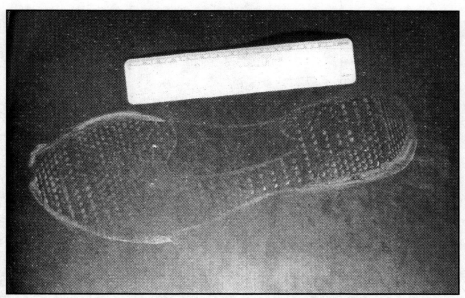

Dusty footwear impression left on a vinyl chair — nearly invisible to the naked eye, this impression was photographed using a low oblique light angle. Photograph by Joe Brown, University of California Davis Police Dept.

Dusty footwear impressions are sometimes found at crime scenes. They can sometimes be detected by shining a strong light source at low oblique angles across surfaces such as floors, doors (e.g., suspect kicked open a door) and victims' bodies (e.g., victim was stomped to death). This type of footwear impression is best photographed with light from a low oblique angle.

Dusty footwear impressions can also be collected with gelatin lifters, static dust lifting materials, and electrostatic dust lifters. Each of these techniques causes the dust to adhere to the lifting medium. Once the dust impression has been lifted, the impression is usually preserved with photography. When photographing a lifted dust impression, position the camera with its film plane parallel to the dust impression, place a scale on the same plane as the impression, and photograph with light from a low oblique angle.

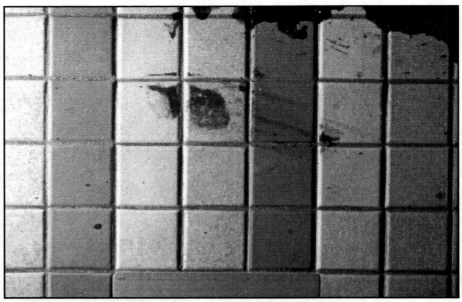

This bloody footwear impression was clearly visible without adding electronic flash and was photographed with ambient light.

Impressions in materials such as blood, grease and oil, which are visible with existing light, may be photographed with ambient (existing) light or with indirect electronic flash (the flash is not pointed directly at the impression). However, it is always best to "preview the photograph" by looking at lighting from several different angles as well as the result of ambient light. To do this, position a strong light source, such as a powerful flashlight, at different angles to find the light angles that show the best detail in the impression. As you move the flashlight, you will see the results you will get by looking into your viewfinder.

Tire Impressions

The technique for photographing a tire impression is similar to photographing footwear impressions. However, you must photograph tire impressions in enough sections to show one circumference of the tire. Place a long scale or tape measure alongside the tire impression. The numbers on the scale must be large enough to be clearly seen in the photograph. Take three or four overlapping photographs to show enough tire impression for one full circumference of the tire. Do not move the scale while taking the photographs. Later, the series of overlapping photographs can be pieced together by matching the scale in the photographs.

Take overlapping photographs to show one circumference of the tire.

When photographing tire impressions remember to use the same techniques of lighting and camera and scale placement as discussed earlier for footwear impressions.

TOOL MARKS

Tool marks are often found at crime scenes. They can be marks left from pry tools, such as crowbars and screwdrivers, marks on a doorknob left from adjustable pliers used to gain entry in a burglary, or other tools used in the commission of a crime. When a tool mark is collected, it is possible that a positive identification can be made linking a tool to the crime.

Tool mark evidence can be collected by casting and by photography. Photographs of tool marks are often used to make positive identifications, but casting of tool marks yields the best evidence. This is because a tool mark is three-dimensional and casting preserves three-dimensional evidence. Casting of tool marks is done with casting putty. At major crime scenes, tool marks should be both casted and photographed. At minor crime scenes, tool marks should be photographed even if it is decided not to cast the tool marks.

In some cases, an item bearing a tool mark can be collected as evidence (e.g., a doorknob bearing marks from pliers is removed from the door and placed into evidence). If the item will be collected, its location should be documented with photographs. Later, close-up photographs and casting of the tool marks can be done in the laboratory.

A mid-range photograph is taken to show the location of a tool mark.

Tool mark evidence photographs must include a scale on the same plane as the tool mark.

When taking a photograph of a tool mark, begin with a photograph to show where the tool mark is located in the crime scene. It may be necessary to use both overview and mid-range photographs to clearly show the location of the tool mark in the photographs. If there are multiple tool marks it may be necessary include numbered evidence markers to differentiate one tool mark from another.

When taking a close-up photograph of a tool mark be sure to place a scale on the same plane as the tool mark. Self-adhesive scales are convenient for photographing tool marks, especially tool marks on vertical surfaces, but a lightweight plastic scale can be taped (using fingerprint tape) to a vertical surface when necessary.

Position the camera with the camera's film plane parallel to the tool mark evidence. In order to get as much detail recorded on the film as possible, position the camera so the frame of the viewfinder is filled with the tool mark and scale. Using a tripod helps with the positioning of the camera and steadies the camera. This is important since depth-of-field is shallow in close-up photographs. Precise focusing can be made with a camera mounted on a tripod. It is best to photograph tool mark evidence with black-and-white film. Black-and-white film provides more contrast and detail than most color films.

Proper lighting will show detail in the tool mark. Do not attempt to photograph tool marks with an electronic flash positioned on the camera. If you do you will normally get reflection from the object you are photographing. The reflection will obscure detail. The best way to light tool marks is with oblique lighting. Oblique lighting will reduce reflections and show greater detail by creating small shadows within the tool marks. The most effective way to ensure you are using the best angles of lighting is "preview the photograph" by looking at lighting from several different angles. To do this, position a strong light source, such as a flashlight, at different angles to find the light angles that reveal the best detail in the tool mark. As you move the lighting, you will see the results you will get by looking into your viewfinder. At this point, you can photograph the tool mark using the lighting from the flashlight or you can position your electronic flash at the best angles for the photographs.

FINGERPRINTS

Perhaps the most common form of evidence collected at crime scenes is fingerprints. Fingerprints should be photographed before they are collected on major cases or if the latent print may be destroyed when lifting.

Photography can also be used to bring out detail in a latent fingerprint. Through the use of lighting, filters and processing controls, a faint latent fingerprint can be enhanced. This is done by building contrast between the latent print and its background.

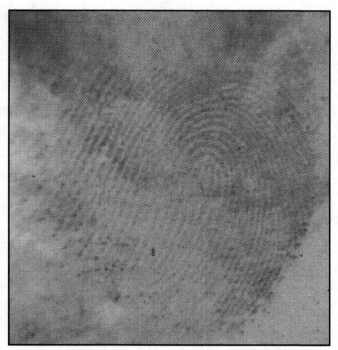

Normal black-and-white film was used to photograph this faint, dusted fingerprint.

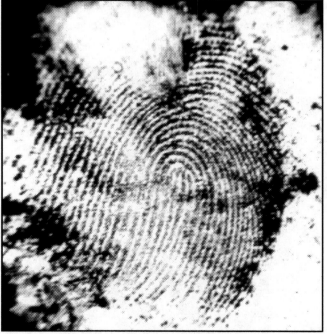

High contrast film was used to photograph the same faint, dusted fingerprint.

Well-defined fingerprints can usually be photographed with color film. However, black-and-white film provides greater contrast than color film and is preferred for latent print photography. The following is a list of a few black-and-white films that are suitable for latent fingerprint photography.

Normal contrast photographs can be taken using a professional black-and-white film such as Kodak T-MAX or Ilford Delta Professional films. For best results develop Kodak T-MAX film in T-MAX developer and process Ilford Delta Professional films in ILFOTEC HC developer. A little higher contrast can be obtained by increasing the film development time by 25%.

High contrast photographs can be taken with Kodak Technical PAN 2415 film. Kodak Technical PAN film has a variable contrast range (high to low contrast) and a variable film speed of ISO 25 to 320. For high contrast, expose Kodak Technical PAN film at ISO 200 and develop the film in Kodak Dektol developer.

Some black-and-white films can be processed in color processing machines. You can take these films to color photo labs for processing in their color equipment. Kodak Professional BW400CN and Ilford XP-2 Super are black-and-white films that are processed in color processors. They each have an ISO of 400, are fine grain with good sharpness and resolution, and are processed in C-41 color chemistry.

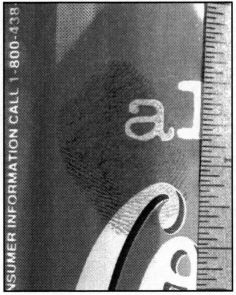

Without any filter - the background and fingerprint record

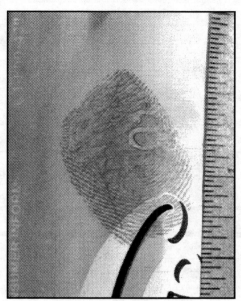

With red filter - the red filter transmits the red
background providing needed contrast

In black-and-white photographs, all colors become shades of gray.
This can be a problem when two colors become nearly the same shade of
gray in a photograph. However, colored filters can be used to increase
contrast between colors in black-and-white photographs. Color filters
can build contrast by either lightening or darkening the latent print, or by
lightening or darkening the background. To lighten a color, the color
filter closest to the color is used. To darken a color, the opposite color
filter is used. (See the following two tables for information on using
filters.)

For example, a black powdered latent on a blue background would
be difficult to see in a black-and-white photograph. However, the latent
print can be enhanced by causing the background to lighten by using a
blue filter. A ninhydrin-developed latent on the back of U.S. currency
can be enhanced in two ways by using a green filter. The green ink in the
currency is lightened (the background is lightened) and the violet
colored ninhydrin developed latent fingerprint is darkened.

Figure 8.1 Filter Table 1

Filter Color	Filter Number	Absorbs (Darkens)	Transmits (Lightens)
Red	25A, 29	Blue & Green - Cyan	Red
Blue	47, 47B	Red & Green - Yellow	Blue
Green	58, 61	Red & Blue - Magenta	Green
Magenta	CC50M	Green	Red & Blue - Magenta
Cyan	CC50C	Red	Blue & Green - Cyan
Yellow	8, 15	Blue	Red & Green - Yellow

Figure 8.2 Filter Table 2

Black and white panchromatic film	
Desired Photographic Result	**Filters used to obtain result**
Blue as black	Red (25, 29)
Blue as white	Blue (47, 47B)
Blue-green as white	Cyan (50C)
Blue-green as black	Red (25, 29)
Green as white	Green (58, 61)
Green as black	Red (25,29) or blue (47,47B)
Orange as black	Blue (47, 47B)
Orange as white	Yellow (15) or red (25, 29)
Red as black	Blue (47, 47B)
Red as white	Red (25, 29)
Violet as black	Green (58, 61)
Violet as white	Blue (47, 47B)
Yellow as black	Blue (47, 47B)
Yellow as white	Yellow (15)
Yellow-green as black	Blue (47, 47B)
Yellow-green as white	Green (58, 61)

NOTE: Colors of objects are hardly ever "pure." The effects described above are never perfect but the direction indicated is correct.

Procedures in Photographing Fingerprints

Establish the Location of the Fingerprint

If you are going to photograph a fingerprint, the location of the fingerprint must be established. While you could use mid-range photographs to show where each fingerprint is located in the scene, the use of numerous mid-range photographs to show the locations of small items can become confusing. A better technique is to forego the mid-range photographs and use the diagram and notations on the latent print card to identify the original location of each fingerprint. This can be done by including a scale in the close-up photograph of each fingerprint. On the scale, write the evidence item number that will be used on the latent print card. Be sure the scale and the item number appear in the close-up photograph of the fingerprint. Then the location of the fingerprint in a photograph can be related to a latent print card on which the fingerprint's location was diagramed and described.

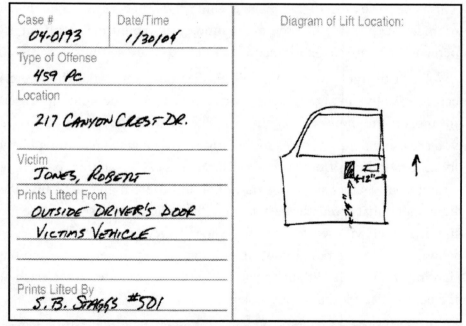

The diagram and notes on a latent print card identify the original location of the fingerprint.

Close-Up Photography

While there are specialized cameras designed for fingerprints, a 35 mm or good quality digital camera with a macro lens or close-up accessory can be used for fingerprint photography. Using a tripod helps with the positioning of the camera and steadies the camera. This is important since depth-of-field is shallow in close-up photographs. Precise focusing can be made with a camera mounted on a tripod. Photograph the latent print with the camera's film plane parallel to the fingerprint surface. In order to get as much detail recorded on the film as possible, position the camera so the frame of your viewfinder is filled with the fingerprint and scale.

Exposure

Some fingerprints can be photographed using ambient (existing) light. Ambient light exposures of fingerprints with normal contrast can be exposed using the camera's exposure system if the fingerprint and its background is of normal reflectance. If the background is lighter or darker than normal, then the exposure should be determined by metering off an 18 percent gray card. For example, when photographing a black powdered fingerprint on a white background the camera will normally underexpose the photograph and detail in the photograph will be lost. This is because most of the image is white and reflects more light than a normal background. In such a situation, you should meter off an 18 percent gray card to determine the correct exposure settings.

Artificial light (from electronic flash, flood lamps, flashlight, etc.) can be effective in photographing fingerprints. Oblique lighting is used for most photographs of fingerprints. The most effective way to ensure you are using the best angles of lighting is "preview the photograph" by looking at lighting from several different angles. To do this, position a strong light source, such as a flashlight, at different angles to find the light angles that reveal the best detail in the fingerprint. As you move the lighting, you will see the results you will get by looking into your viewfinder. At this point, you can photograph the fingerprint using the lighting from the flashlight or you can position your electronic flash at the best angles for the photographs.

Whether using available light, electronic flash, or other illumination sources, bracketing of exposures should be considered. Bracketing may reveal more detail in "low contrast" or faint fingerprints. Underexposing the film will separate the steps on the white end of the gray scale. Overexposure will separate the steps on the black-end of the gray scale. The latitude for black-and-white film is generally two stops underexposure and six stops overexposure.

Photographing Specific Types of Fingerprint Subjects

Dusted fingerprints with good visible detail can usually be photographed without special lighting techniques.

Fingerprint impressions in soft substances (e.g., wax, putty, clay, adhesive tape, grease, or dust) require the use of oblique lighting at a low angle. This will create small shadows in the impression. Preview the effect with a flashlight.

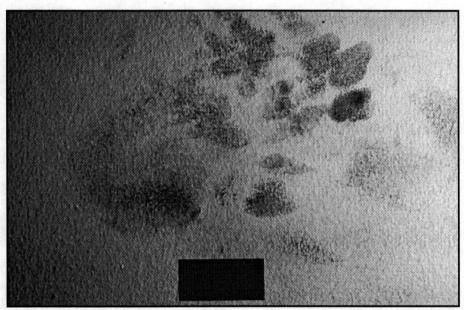

In this photograph of palm prints the oblique angle of the flash was too low, creating shadows in the textured wall covering. The shadows obscure the friction ridge detail of the palm print.

Fingerprints on porous surfaces (textured wall coverings, wood, brick, etc.) may need almost a 90-degree lighting angle to avoid the creation of shadows in the surface's texture, which would interfere with the recording of fingerprint detail. Preview the effect with a flashlight.

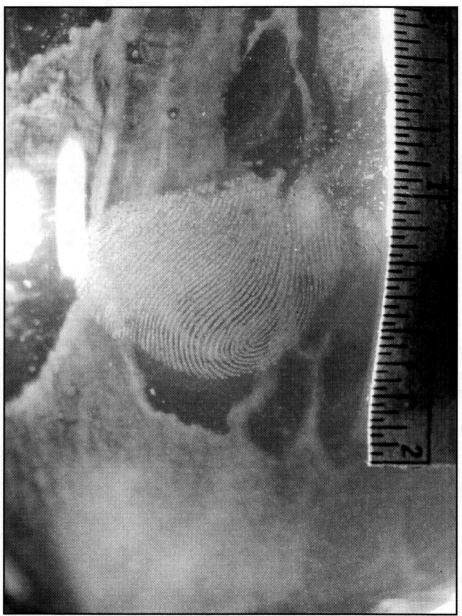

Fingerprint on drinking glass using transmitted lighting - position a diffused light source behind the glass.

Fingerprints on glass (windows, drinking glasses, etc.) can be photographed by placing a white card behind the glass and using a low oblique angle of light. They can also be photographed by using transmitted (back) lighting by positioning a diffused light source behind the glass.

BLOODSTAIN PHOTOGRAPHY

Bloodstain (also referred to as blood-spatter) at a crime scene can tell the story of what occurred during an assault or other type of bloody crime scene. Bloodstain analysis can determine such things as where victims and suspects were positioned when bloody blows occurred and events during the assault (e.g., which victim bled first). The crime scene photographer is responsible for photographically documenting a bloodstain scene in such detail that a bloodstain expert can later do an analysis of the bloodstain evidence. These photographs will include areas of bloodstain that indicate a pattern. An example of a pattern area is shown in the photograph below.

Many photographs of bloodstains will include areas that indicate a pattern. This photograph shows the direction bloodstain, mostly arterial spurting, traveled and struck a bathroom partition.

When photographing bloodstain scenes use color film to establish which substances in the photograph are bloodstains. Black-and-white film records reflected light in shades of gray, so when using black-and-white film it may be difficult to determine what substances in the photography are actually bloodstains.

Black-and-white film may be used for high contrast photographs or with colored filters to increase contrast between the background and bloodstain. For example, if a bloodstain is located on a dark surface, you can use black-and-white film and a red filter to lighten the bloodstain, or if a bloodstain is located on a light surface, you can use black-and-white film and a blue filter to darken the bloodstain.

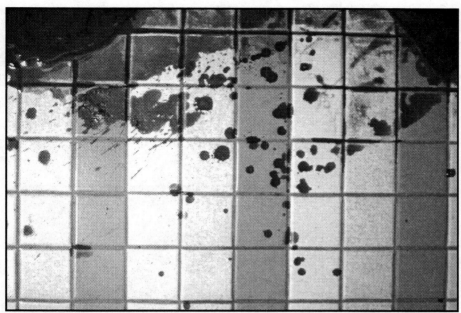

When photographing bloodstain evidence, use a scale on the same plane as the bloodstain and photograph with the film plane parallel to the plane of the bloodstain. Use oblique lighting.

When photographing bloodstains you must first show the location of the bloodstain with mid-range photographs followed with closer views to show the bloodstain patterns. When taking close-up photographs of bloodstains be sure to place a scale on the same plane as the bloodstain. Self-adhesive scales are convenient for photographing small areas, especially vertical surfaces, but a lightweight plastic scale can be taped (using fingerprint tape) to a vertical surface when necessary.

Position the camera with the camera's film plane parallel to the bloodstain evidence. In order to get as much detail recorded on the film as possible, your camera should be positioned so the frame of your viewfinder is filled with the bloodstain and scale. Using a tripod helps with the positioning of the camera and steadies the camera. This is important since depth-of-field is shallow in close-up photographs. Precise focusing can be made with a camera mounted on a tripod.

Proper lighting will show the detail of the bloodstain patterns and evidence. Do not attempt to photograph bloodstain with an electronic flash positioned on the camera. If you do you will normally get reflection from the surface you are photographing. The reflection will obscure detail. The best way to light bloodstain is with oblique lighting. Oblique lighting will reduce reflections and show greater detail in the evidence. Use very low oblique light angles when dealing with bloodstain on fabrics. The most effective way to ensure you are using the best angles of lighting is "preview the photograph" by looking at lighting from several different angles. To do this, position a strong light source, such as a flashlight, at different angles to find the light angles that reveal the best detail in the tool mark. As you move the lighting, you will see the results you will get by looking into your viewfinder. Position your electronic flash at the best angles for the photographs.

Photographs are taken to document strings that demonstrate the origin of bloodstains.

Some investigators will use strings to determine the origin of bloodstain at a crime scene. The origin is usually the location of a bloody blow in an assault. The technique involves measuring a group of blood drops on a surface, such as a wall, to find the angle the each drop of blood was traveling when it struck the surface. Strings are attached to the points each blood drop struck and the strings are then angled back to an approximate point of origin. Photographs are then taken to document the demonstration.

Photographs can also be taken to illustrate theories involving bloodstain evidence, such as the position of a victim at the time of a bloody blow. In the illustrations below, photographs are used to show the approximate location of the victim's head at the time of a bloody blow. The first photograph shows an area of the floor that has a "shadow." The shadow is an area without bloodstain. This shadow was caused when a partition blocked bloodstain that traveled through the air from the point of origin. The second photograph was taken without moving the camera, but with the electronic flash positioned where it was believed the victim's head was located when the bloody blow occurred. The second photograph shows an actual shadow caused by the partition.

The photographer sets up his camera to photograph the floor area where a "shadow" is located.

Photograph #1 shows the "shadow" area on the floor.

The photographer positions the electronic flash where it is believed the victim's head was located.

These two photographs can be used in court to help illustrate the testimony given by a bloodstain expert regarding the position of the victim's head at the time of the bloody blow.

Photograph #2 shows an actual shadow due to the position of the flash.

Photographing Luminol

Luminol is a presumptive test for blood usually used to reveal bloodstain patterns on surfaces where the bloodstain has been cleaned or is not readily visible. Luminol reacts with the iron in hemoglobin causing the area with traces of blood to become luminescent. The luminescence is documented with photography. Other chemiluminescent chemicals, such as fluorescein, can be used in a similar manner.

When photographing luminol you will need a camera with a "B" setting, a lens with a f/1.8 or larger aperture, a locking cable release, a tripod, an electronic flash, a roll of ISO 400 color print film, and a timer.

Take a normal photograph of the area before taking the luminol photograph.

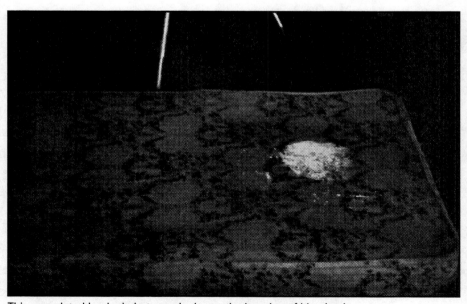

This completed luminol photograph shows the location of bloodstain.

To photograph the results of luminol inside a building, you would first turn off lights in the area and spray a fine mist of a luminol solution over the area to be searched. If luminescence is observed, note its location. Next, turn on the room lights. Set up a camera, equipped with a locking cable release and an electronic flash, on a tripod. Take a normal photograph of the area. Without moving the camera, advance the film and adjust the lens aperture to underexpose the next photograph by two f/stops. This can be done with an automatic camera by adjusting the exposure control setting (to a setting of -2) or with a manual camera by closing down the lens aperture (e.g., if the normal flash photograph requires a f/5.6, change the aperture to f/11). Set the shutter speed to "B." With the room darkened, open the shutter (firing the electronic flash) and lock the cable release to hold open the shutter. Open the lens aperture all the way while taking care not to move the camera. Lightly spray luminol on the area in the view of the camera, and then re-spray the area every twenty seconds to maintain luminescence. Avoid over-spraying, which may cause patterns on smooth surfaces to run or may cause background luminescence and reduce needed contrast. Close the shutter after about one minute.

A scale can be used in the luminol photograph. Attach small pieces of copper wire on the one-inch marks of a scale and place the scale in the area to be photographed. The copper wire on the scale will become luminescent when sprayed with Luminol.

BULLET PATH PHOTOGRAPHY

The suspected path of a bullet can be illustrated with a variety of techniques. Colored strings can be strung to illustrate bullet paths. Reflective string can also be used—the string will glow when a flash photograph is taken. Fiberglass rods or wooden dowels can also be used, especially to show how a bullet passed through an object or wall. With these techniques, you will need to set up the strings or rods and photograph the area from several angles to document the bullet paths.

Another technique for photographing the suspected path of a bullet is to use a laser beam. As with the other techniques, the bullet paths illustrated with laser beams are documented with photographs.

When photographing a bullet path illustrated with a laser, you will need a camera with a "B" setting, a lens with f/1.8 or larger aperture, a locking cable release, a tripod, an electronic flash, a roll of ISO 400 color print film, and a laser.

Bullet path photography using a laser beam reflected off a white card.

To photograph a bullet path using a laser, you first position the laser to illustrate the suspected bullet path. Then set up a camera, equipped with a locking cable release and an electronic flash, on a tripod. Adjust the lens aperture to underexpose the photograph by one or two f/stops. This can be done with an automatic camera by adjusting the exposure control setting (to a setting of -1 or -2) or with a manual camera by closing down the lens aperture (e.g., if the normal flash photograph requires a f/5.6, change the aperture to f/8 or f/11). Set the shutter speed to "B." Turn on the laser. With the room darkened, open the shutter (firing the electronic flash) and lock the cable release to hold open the shutter. Open the lens aperture all the way while taking care not to move the camera. Cause the laser beam path to show in the photograph by either spraying photographic fog in the path of the laser beam, or by slowly moving a white card along the laser beam path with the card positioned so the laser dot on the card reflects toward the camera. When you finish tracing the laser beam path, return to the camera and close the shutter.

SUMMARY

This chapter has given you a variety of techniques for photographing some of the more common types of evidence found at crime scenes. However, crime scene conditions and types of evidence vary greatly from one crime scene to the next. To successfully photograph evidence you must be experienced and knowledgeable in both photography and forensics, be willing to experiment with lighting, be a problem solver, and be creative.

DISCUSSION QUESTIONS

1. If we agree that casting a footwear impression provides better evidence than a photo, why do we take photos of an impression before casting?

2. How can the location and orientation of an impression be documented if the impression is located in an area without recognizable landmarks?

3. Describe how you would position the camera, scale, and electronic flash to photograph a dusty footwear impression.

4. How can tool mark evidence be collected?

5. Under what circumstances would you usually decide to photograph a fingerprint before it is lifted?

6. When using black-and-white film, all colors become shades of gray. What technique can you use to lighten the shade of gray for a specific color?

7. Describe how you can document the location of a fingerprint without using photographs.

8. Describe how you would photograph a fingerprint on a brick wall.

9. Why is it necessary to photograph the results of using luminol at a crime scene?

10. What does luminol react with to become luminescent?

EXERCISES AND ACTIVITIES

1. In soft soil, create a footwear or tire impression to simulate a crime scene. Take three photographs of the impression: one to establish location, a close-up and one with a scale on the same plane as the impression.

2. Take a series of photographs with the electronic flash or light source at six different angles.

3. Simulate a crime scene with an impression on a dusty surface. It may be nearly invisible to the naked eye. Photograph the impression using the low oblique light technique.

4. Take overlapping photographs to show the circumference of a tire.

5. Create a tool mark on a piece of scrape or other material that can be discarded. Take mid-range and close-up photographs of the tool mark.

ADDITIONAL RESOURCES

Bodziak, William J., (1999) *Footwear Impression Evidence: Detection, Recovery and Examination*, Second Edition, CRC Press, Boca Raton, Florida 33431

Byrd, Mike, (2001) *Crime Scene Evidence: A Guide to the Recovery and Collection of Physical Evidence*, Staggs Publishing, Wildomar, California 92595

Champod, Christophe; Lennard, Chris J,; Margot, Pierre; Stoilovic, Milutin; (2004) *Fingerprints and Other Ridge Skin Impressions*, CRC Press, Boca Raton, Florida 33431

Duckworth, John E., (1983) *Forensic Photography*, Charles C. Thomas, Springfield, Illinois 62717

Fisher, Barry A. J., (2003) *Techniques of Crime Scene Investigation*, Seventh Edition, CRC Press, Boca Raton, Florida 33431

Garrison Jr., Dean H., (2003) *Practical Shooting Scene Investigation: The Investigation and Reconstruction of Crime Scenes Involving Gunfire*, Universal Publishers, Boca Raton, FL 33486

Hilderbrand, Dwane S., (1999) *Footwear, The Missed Evidence: A Field Guide to the Collection and Preservation of Forensic Footwear Impression Evidence*, Staggs Publishing, Wildomar, California 92595

James, Stuart, (1998) *Interpretation of Bloodstain Evidence at Crime Scenes*, Second Edition, CRC Press, Boca Raton, Florida 33431

McDonald, James A., (1992) *Close-up and Macro Photography for Evidence Technicians*, Second Edition, Phototext Books, Palatine, Illinois 60067

Miller, Larry S., (1998) *Police Photography*, Fourth Edition, Anderson Publishing Co., Cincinnati, Ohio 45202

Staggs, Steven, (2005) *Crime Scene and Evidence Photographer's Guide*, Second Edition, Staggs Publishing, Wildomar, California 92595

Chapter 9

Evidence Photography In The Laboratory

CHAPTER OVERVIEW

Often evidence must be transported to the laboratory for processing. The evidence may require scientific analysis. It may require specialized photography requiring controlled lighting or specialized techniques that cannot be accomplished at the crime scene.

CHAPTER OBJECTIVES

At the end of this chapter you will be understand the basics of laboratory photography and how to photograph several types of evidence in the laboratory including:

1. Serial numbers
2. Forensic light source photography
3. Ultraviolet photography
4. Infrared photography
5. Clothing and other evidence examinations
6. Microscopes
7. Matching photographs
8. Exhibits

INTRODUCTION TO EVIDENCE PHOTOGRAPHY IN THE LABORATORY

As you study this chapter, be aware that many of the laboratory techniques in this chapter can also be applied at the crime scene. For example, most forensic light sources are portable and are often used for searching for certain types of evidence at the crime scene. It is possible that some forensic light source photography will have to be completed at the crime scene, especially if the evidence cannot be moved (e.g., evidence on a fixed object or surface). Also, some crime scene photographers prefer to set up portable copy stands and use laboratory techniques at the crime scene so they can photograph as much evidence as possible at the scene, reducing the need to collect some items as evidence. For example, during the investigation of a residential burglary, blood is found at the point of entry (a broken window). The victim of the burglary points out an antique vase that was moved during the crime. The investigator finds blood on the vase that may have been transferred there from the suspect. The investigator could collect the vase as evidence, but the vase would need to be returned to the victim after photography and blood collection was completed at the laboratory. Instead, the investigator may elect to set up a portable copy stand at the scene, photograph the vase and bloodstain, and collect the bloodstain evidence. The vase can then be left at the scene. It is up to the crime scene investigator to determine the best course of action for each item of evidence.

LABORATORY CAMERA EQUIPMENT

Much of the photography done in the laboratory is accomplished with a dedicated copy camera or with a 35 mm camera attached to a camera stand. These devices have lighting attachments and camera height adjustments to facilitate controlled lighting and accurate focusing.

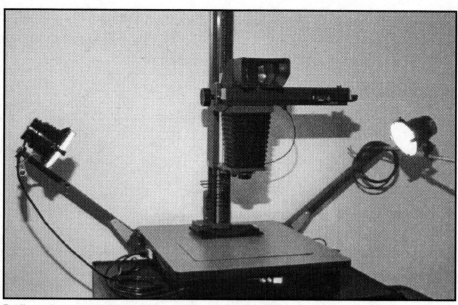

Dedicated copy camera used for evidence photography.

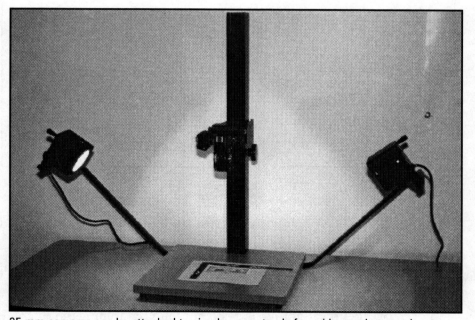

35 mm cameras can be attached to simple copy stands for evidence photography.

Lighting Methods for Copy and Evidence Close-up Photography

Since most laboratory photography is made with steady burning lights (quartz lamps, photoflood lamps, fluorescent lamps, etc.) it is relatively easy to choose the best lighting method for photographing a specific item of evidence. All you need to do is try different lighting methods while looking in the camera's viewfinder, and select the method that gives the best results. The following lighting methods are effective for photographing various evidence subjects.

45-degree Lighting

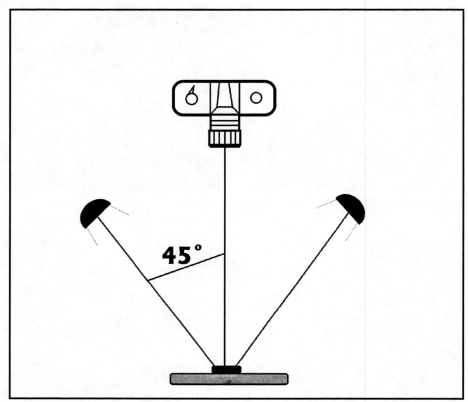

45-degree Lighting

Forty-five degree lighting uses one or more lights positioned at 45-degree angles. If only one light is used, a white or silver reflector can be placed on the opposite side of the evidence to reflect some of the light back toward the evidence, reducing shadows.

Forty-five degree lighting is used for photographing the average item of evidence where the objective is to show the item's shape and size.

Direct Reflective Lighting

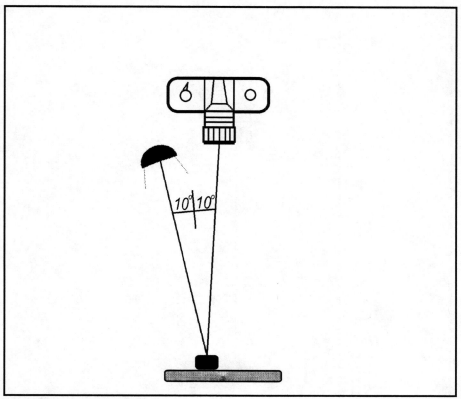

Direct Reflective Lighting

In direct reflective lighting, the light is reflected directly off the subject into the lens. This is done by placing the subject at a 10-degree angle from the lens to film plane and placing the light source at 10-degree angle from the subject. The light source reflects at a 20-degree angle into the lens.

Direct reflective lighting is used to minimize shadows within the evidence. However, this method creates very high contrast and does not show the dimensional shape or texture of the evidence. In addition, the light source may need to be diffused to prevent hot spots.

Oblique Lighting

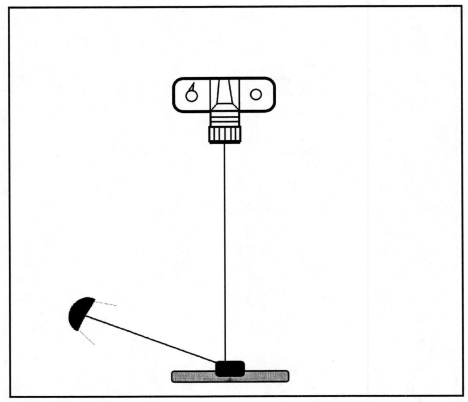

Oblique Lighting

Oblique lighting uses a light source positioned at a low angle. Oblique lighting is usually used to show detail by creating shadows in the surface of the evidence. It is commonly used when photographing impressions, tool marks and certain types of fingerprints. A very low oblique angle of lighting can be used to photograph dusty footwear impressions and indented writing.

Bounce Lighting

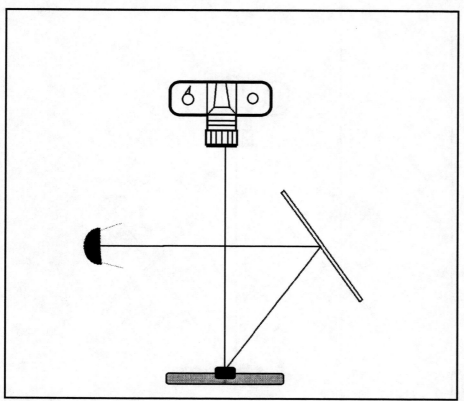

Bounce Lighting

Bounce lighting uses light bounced off a white or reflective surface. The bounce surface may be positioned at different locations (above or to one side of the subject) to create the desired effect. This usually produces even non-glare lighting with low contrast.

Diffused Lighting

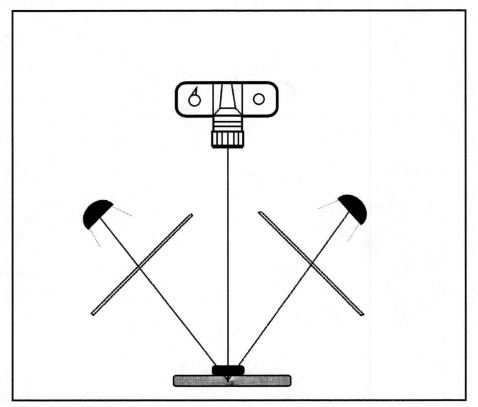

Diffused Lighting

Diffused lighting uses an opaque material placed between the light source and the subject to soften the light. This usually results in even lighting with reduced reflections and hot spots. The opaque material can be as simple as a section of a white bed sheet or an empty water bottle, or can be a commercial device designed for laboratory photography.

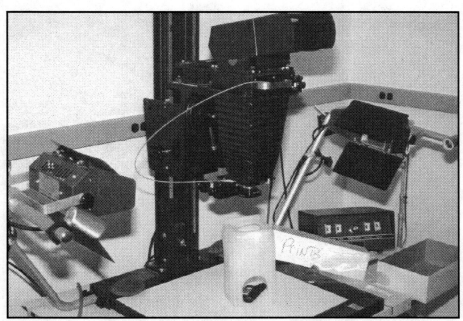

A white plastic water bottle was used to diffuse the light and reduce reflections when photographing a fingerprint on a small handgun.

The Cloud Dome, a commercial device designed for laboratory photography, is effective for diffusing light.

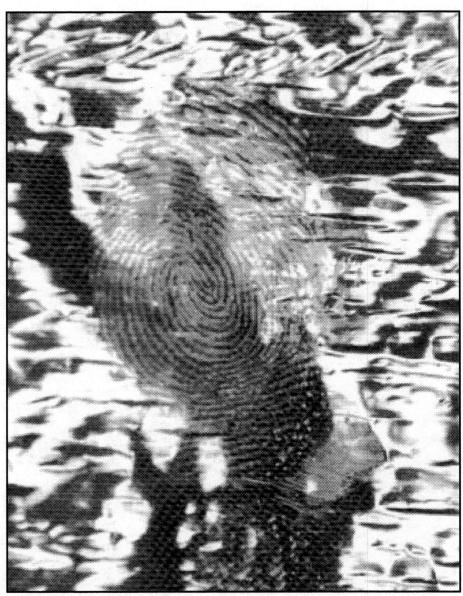

This photograph of a fingerprint on plastic wrap was taken with standard 45—degree lighting. Reflections on the plastic wrap obscure the detail in the fingerprint.

This photograph of a fingerprint on plastic wrap was taken using the diffused lighting provided by the Cloud Dome. The diffused lighting eliminates most reflections.

Diffused lighting is usually used for photographing evidence with shiny or reflective surfaces.

Transmitted Lighting

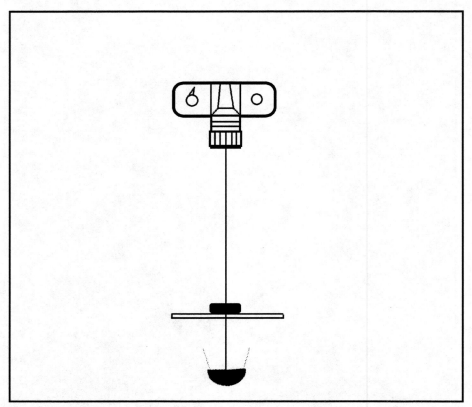

Transmitted Lighting

Transmitted lighting uses light that shines through the evidence toward the camera's lens, and the background becomes shadow-free. The angle of the transmitted lighting can be adjusted from 90-degrees to 45-degrees for the desired effect.

Transmitted lighting is used for photographing transparent or translucent subjects. It is effective in photographing evidence such as fingerprints on a drinking glass.

Front Directional or Axial Lighting

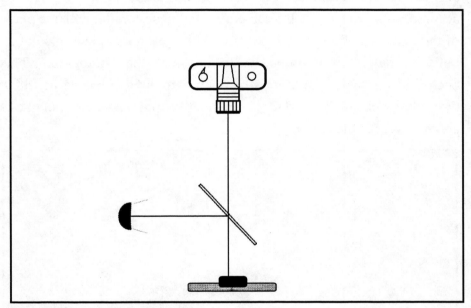

Front Directional or Axial Lighting

Front directional lighting allows you to send light straight down onto the evidence. A clear piece of glass is placed between the subject and lens at a 45-degree angle. The light source is positioned parallel to the film place and 45-degrees to the glass. While the light is transmitted through the glass, some is reflected downward directly on the subject. Front directional lighting is effective when photographing into hollow cavities, such as glasses or cups.

Other Variations of Lighting

Two or more of the lighting methods described above can be used together for lighting evidence. For example, when photographing a broken piece of glass you might use a combination of transmitted lighting and diffused 45-degree lighting.

In addition, mirrors and white or silver reflector cards can be used to reflect light into shadow areas when using the lighting methods previously described. Other devices, such as small spotlights and fiber optic lighting, can be utilized to light small areas.

CAMERA AND SCALE ORIENTATION FOR LABORATORY PHOTOGRAPHS

When taking photographs of evidence you must position the camera and evidence to minimize distortion in the photograph. This can be accomplished by keeping the camera's film plane parallel with the plane of the evidence. Taking a photograph with the camera positioned at an oblique angle will introduce distortion into the photograph. This becomes extremely important when photographing evidence in which the photograph will be used for comparison purposes, such as tool marks and footwear evidence.

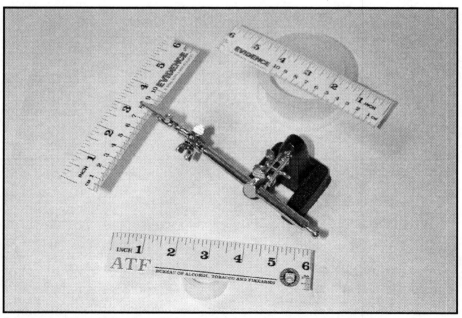

Scales must be positioned on the same plane as the evidence. Scales can be positioned using small stands, blocks of wood, empty tape spools, or other devices.

Scales are used in most laboratory photographs. Scales are required when photographing evidence for comparison purposes (e.g., the sole of a shoe when the photograph will be compared with an impression casted at the scene). When a scale is used in a photograph, the scale must be positioned on the same plane as the evidence. Taking a photograph with the scale on a different plane will introduce distortion into the photograph and the scale will be virtually useless. Scales can be positioned using small stands, blocks of wood, empty tape spools, or other devices.

FOCUSING

When taking close-up photographs one of the most common problems encountered is shallow depth-of-field. Therefore, accurate focusing is critical. One important technique regarding focusing for close-up photography is to avoid focusing on the scale. Instead, be sure to focus on the evidence. While it is frequently easier to focus on the markings or edge of the scale, the scale may not always be on the exact plane of the evidence. It is better to have a sharp image of the evidence and a slightly out of focus scale than to have a sharp image of the scale and the evidence out of focus.

When focusing in the laboratory, it is often easier to move the evidence slightly to bring it into focus than to try to fine focus the lens. A small platform on a scissors jack can be used to raise or lower evidence for focusing.

EXPOSURE

Correct exposure is critical in evidence photography. Incorrect exposures can result in lost detail in a photograph. While electronic flash can also be used in laboratory photography, most evidence photography done in a laboratory setting uses steady burning lamps.

When using steady burning lamps, exposures can be metered either with the camera's internal exposure meter or with an external exposure meter. However, before relying on any reflected light exposure meter, you should determine if the meter will be providing an accurate reading due to the subject or background about to be photographed. Exposure meters use 18 percent reflectance in determining exposure. If you are photographing evidence or a background that does not have 18 percent reflectance then the exposure reading can be in error. For example, when the evidence you are photographing is a dusted fingerprint on a white surface, an exposure meter will, as always, base its exposure settings on 18 percent reflectance. Since the subject matter in the photograph is almost all white, the meter will provide exposure settings that result in an underexposed photograph. Much of the detail in the photograph will be lost. A second example would be a dark item, such as a black revolver. The exposure meter will base its settings on 18 percent reflectance and would provide exposure setting that result in an overexposed photograph. Much of the detail in the revolver will be lost.

When using steady burning lamps for laboratory photographs you can ensure accurate exposures by metering off an 18 percent gray card. Position the 18 percent gray card in front of the exposure meter, or in front of the camera lens if you are using the camera's exposure meter, to obtain the correct exposure settings. Be sure the light is falling on the 18 percent gray card the same as it is falling on your evidence. Use the settings indicated by the exposure meter for the photograph. In many cases, bracketing should also be considered. Bracketing will provide a series of photographs at different exposures. Later, the best exposures from the series of photographs can be used for the investigation.

Normal electronic flash exposures can be done in either automatic or manual flash when photographing evidence. Through-the-lens (TTL) electronic flash unit exposures will be controlled automatically by the camera's TTL flash metering system. When using electronic flash, bracketing should also be considered.

SERIAL NUMBERS

Stamped or engraved serial numbers are photographed using oblique lighting.

When taking close-up photographs of serial numbers, use either 45-degree or oblique lighting, or if the numbers are printed on a label, 45-degree lighting will usually be adequate to document the serial numbers. If the serial numbers are either raised or engraved then oblique lighting would be used to create small shadows in the numbers. The small shadows would make the numbers visible in the photograph.

Serial numbers that have been obliterated or altered must also be documented photographically. Frequently obliterated numbers, usually serial numbers that have been removed by filing, can be restored by forensic scientists. Photographs of the serial numbers should be taken before and after restoration using oblique lighting.

FORENSIC LIGHT SOURCE PHOTOGRAPHY

Forensic light sources, also referred to as alternate light sources, are used both at crime scenes and in the laboratory to detect and document various types of evidence. Forensic light sources vary in design from battery-powered portable units that are designed to search for specific evidence to larger laboratory units with a variety of forensic applications.

Often, evidence is invisible to the naked eye without a forensic light source. Most forensic light sources use interchangeable filters, or a filter wheel, to select the band of light necessary to detect certain evidence. For example, a broadband filter (approximately 45nm) would be used to detect and document evidence such as saliva, semen, urine, bloodstain, fibers, and accelerants. Varieties of narrow band filters are used for enhancing fingerprints that have been revealed with fingerprint powders (including fluorescent powders) and chemical methods.

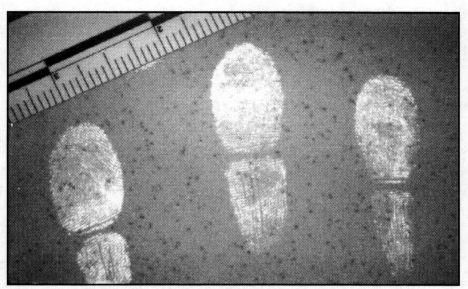

Fingerprints dusted with fluorescent powder and illuminated with a forensic light source. An orange filter was used over the lens.

When using a forensic light source, you wear colored goggles to view the evidence illuminated by the forensic light source. Orange, red and yellow goggles are used depending on the band filter in use. Photography to document the result is relatively easy. When you see the best result with the forensic light source just duplicate what you see for the camera using black-and-white film. If you are wearing orange goggles then shine the forensic light on the evidence and place an orange filter over the camera's lens to take the photograph. Determine a starting exposure with the camera's metering system or a separate light meter. When using a separate light meter, use the filter factor for the band cut off filter to compute the exposure. Bracket exposures by a minimum of two f/stops.

Ultraviolet Photography

Ultraviolet lighting techniques can be used to illuminate body fluids, fluoresce latent prints that have been dusted with fluorescent powders, and to produce high resolution photographs of skin surfaces. It is a good technique for photographing bite marks, cuts, and scratches. Bruises with blood accumulation close to the skin surface can also be photographed with ultraviolet photography.

To photograph using ultraviolet light you will need a camera, high speed black-and-white film and a lens capable of transmitting light between 320nm and 400nm. (Most lenses are designed to prevent excess ultraviolet transmission. A lens can be tested with a spectrophotometer to determine if it can transmit light between 320nm and 400nm.)

There are two types of ultraviolet photography, fluorescent and reflected. Fluorescent ultraviolet photography is accomplished by getting an object to glow, usually by using a "black light," and then photographing it. Fluorescent ultraviolet photography must be done in a darkened room. A starting exposure setting is determined by metering either with the camera's internal exposure meter or with an external exposure meter. Exposures should be bracketed by two f/stops.

Reflected ultraviolet photography is different in that it can be accomplished without darkening the room. A light source rich in ultraviolet light is necessary. Such light sources include tungsten lights, photoflood lights, fluorescent lights and electronic flash. A Kodak Wratten 18A filter is placed over the camera's lens during the exposure. The 18A filter blocks visible light while allowing ultraviolet light to pass through. Exposure settings are determined by evaluating test photographs. You can find a starting point for exposures by using the exposure settings indicated by the camera's internal exposure meter with the filter in place or with an external exposure meter using a filter factor of 80 (+6.5 stops). Exposures should be bracketed by two f/stops.

Some forensic light sources, called Reflected Ultraviolet Imaging Systems (RUVIS) are designed for ultraviolet reflectance viewing and photography. Ultraviolet forensic light sources are frequently used at crime scenes to detect fingerprints on non-porous surfaces prior to any treatment or after a cyanoacrylate (superglue) fuming, footwear impressions on smooth surfaces, explosive residues and for luminol enhancement. Ultraviolet forensic light sources can also be used to enhance injuries including bite marks. A reflected ultraviolet imaging system is a device that consists of an ultraviolet image intensifier, a short-wave ultraviolet bandpass filter, and includes an optical system you look through to see the results. They can be attached to a camera to take ultraviolet photographs.

When taking fluorescent or reflected ultraviolet photographs, be sure to take both white light and ultraviolet light photographs of the evidence. These can be used for comparison and for explaining your technique in court.

Infrared Photography

Infrared photography is useful in analyzing and photographing evidence including questioned documents, gunshot residue, stains, and irregularities in cloth. Infrared films are sensitive to infrared radiation, as well as visible light and some ultraviolet radiation. Infrared films must be handled in total darkness. Cameras must be loaded and unloaded in total darkness to avoid infrared radiation from reaching the film.

To photograph evidence with infrared you will need a camera, lens with an infrared focusing mark, black-and-white infrared film, and a light source.

Infrared focusing mark (indicated by arrow) on a standard lens.

Lenses do not focus infrared radiation on the same plane as visible light. This is because infrared radiation has a longer wavelength than visible light. When focusing for infrared you first focus for visible light without a filter over the lens. Once focused for visible light, the lens is adjusted for infrared by aligning the distance on the lens's focusing scale to the infrared focusing mark.

A Kodak Wratten filter #87 is placed over the lens to block all ultraviolet radiation. Tungsten lamps or electronic flashes are usually used to light the subject.

Because the ratio of infrared radiation to visible light varies, exposure settings are usually determined by test photographs. When using Kodak high-speed infrared film, a starting point for exposures can be determined by setting the ISO on the camera or light meter to ISO 25. If you are using the camera's internal metering system, be sure to take the exposure readings before mounting the filter on the lens. Bracketing should be used when taking infrared photographs. Bracketing will provide a series of photographs at different exposures. Later, the best exposures from the series of photographs can be used for the investigation.

Clothing

Clothing is often collected as evidence. It could be a suspect's clothing with glass fragments, gunshot residue, blood, or other evidence adhered to its surfaces. It could be the victim's clothing containing semen, bloodstain or other evidence. Forensic light sources are often used to search for evidence on clothing.

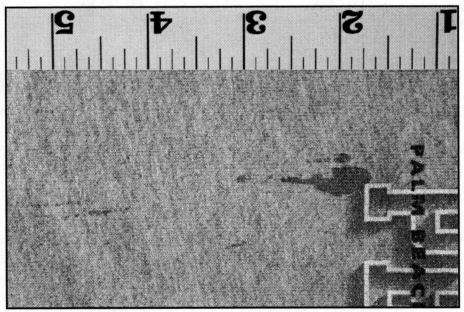

This photograph of bloodstain on a shirt was taken with oblique lighting.

When photographing clothing and evidence found on clothing, lighting will depend on the character of the evidence photographed. Evidence revealed using a forensic light source would be photographed using the forensic light for illumination. Some details in fabrics can be shown with transmitted lighting, others, such as bloodstain, with oblique lighting.

Microscopes

Some types of evidence may be analyzed in the laboratory utilizing microscopes. Some microscope systems are designed for making tool mark or ballistics comparisons. Most microscopes in crime laboratories have attachments for cameras. Others have digital cameras designed into the microscope for both viewing and photography.

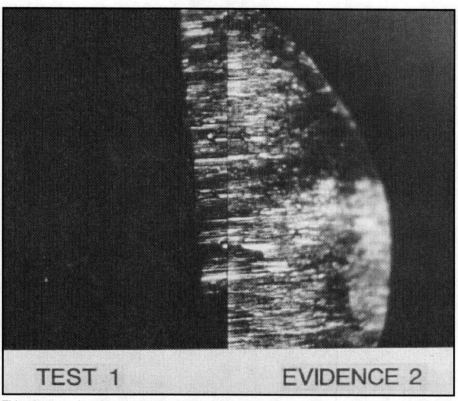

This photograph, taken through a comparison microscope, shows a match between a cut padlock and a test cut made with bolt cutters found in a suspect's possession.

When photographing evidence through a microscope you can determine a starting exposure with the camera's metering system. Bracketing will provide a series of photographs at different exposures. Later, the best exposures from the series of photographs can be used for the investigation.

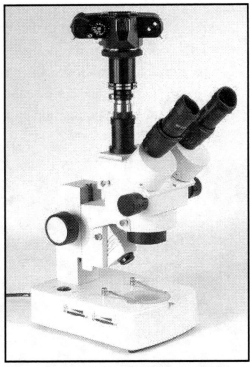

Most microscopes in crime laboratories have attachments for cameras.

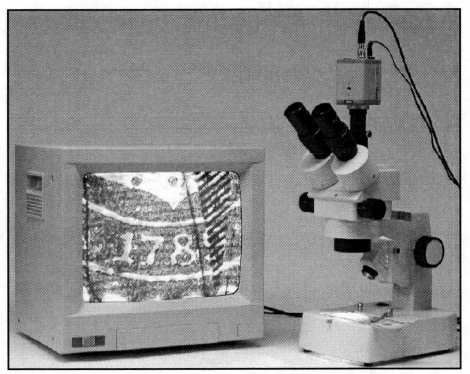

Some microscopes have integrated digital cameras for both viewing and photography.

Matching Photographs

A common type of laboratory photography is the "matching photograph." The purpose of a matching photograph is to visibly illustrate that two pieces of evidence were at one time joined together. For example, a physical match is made with two pieces of headlight glass, one found at the collision scene and one on the hit-and-run suspect's vehicle. Photographs are made to illustrate the match. Other matches could be two pieces of torn clothing or a paper match torn from a matchbook.

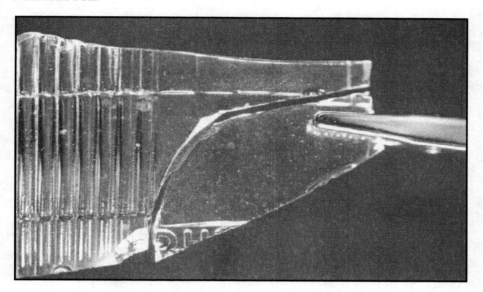

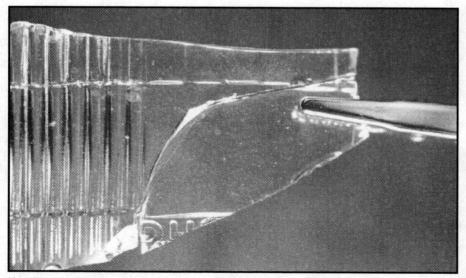

Usually two photographs are taken to illustrate a physical match. One photograph is taken with a space between the two pieces and the second is taken with the two pieces joined.

Another type of matching photograph is an illustration that one object touched or impacted another object. For example, a pry tool in the suspect's possession is determined to be the tool that made a mark on a doorjamb. At some point in the investigation, a matching photograph may be taken. However, be certain matching photographs are only taken after trace evidence, if any, is collected from both objects. Otherwise, the positioning the two pieces of evidence together will cross-contaminate the evidence. In this example, wood fibers and paint found on the pry tool could match the doorjamb.

Usually two photographs are taken to illustrate a physical match. One photograph is taken with a space between the two pieces and the second is taken with the two pieces joined.

Lighting for the matching photographs will depend on the character of the evidence photographed. A combination of transmitted and diffused lighting was used in the above example photographs of a headlight glass match.

EXHIBITS

Often exhibits will need to be prepared for illustrating testimony in court. Many exhibits are simply photographs from the crime scene or of evidence. These photographs can be used to help the court and jury understand the crime and the conclusions reached by the investigators.

Another type of exhibit is one that can be used to demonstrate the conclusions regarding evidence. In the series of photographs below, an exhibit is constructed to demonstrate how the suspect's shoe matches a footwear impression found at a crime scene.

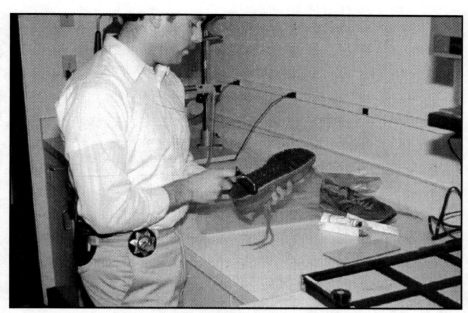

Fingerprint ink is rolled across the sole of the suspect's shoe.

The ink is transferred from the shoe sole to a clear sheet of plastic.

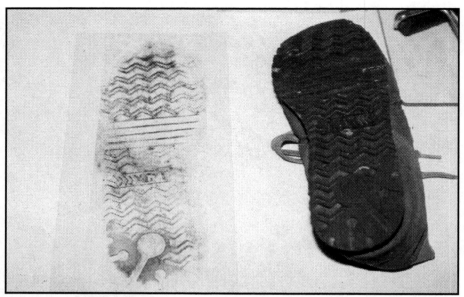

This produces a life-sized (1:1) transparency of the shoe sole.

A life-sized (1:1) photographic print of the shoe impression is made by matching the scale in the photograph with a scale placed on the easel.

The transparency and photograph can be displayed to the court and jury.

The transparency is placed over the photograph to illustrate the match.

SUMMARY

This chapter has given you a variety of techniques for photographing evidence in a laboratory setting. Photographs are ideal for illustrating an investigator's testimony about evidence. To successfully photograph evidence you must be experienced and knowledgeable in both photography and forensics, be willing to experiment with lighting, be a problem solver, and be creative.

DISCUSSION QUESTIONS

1. What are the seven lighting methods for copy and evidence close-up photography?

2. What types of evidence are best photographed with oblique lighting?

3. What devices or materials can you use to diffuse light when photographing a shiny or reflective item of evidence?

4. What color filter do you use on the camera's lens when photographing evidence with a forensic light source?

5. What evidence would a forensic light source with a broadband filter detect?

6. What evidence would a forensic light source with a narrow band filter detect?

7. When using a forensic light source and wearing orange goggles, what filter would you place over the camera's lens for photography?

8. Explain the differences between fluorescent ultraviolet photography and reflected ultraviolet photography.

9. How do you focus the camera when taking infrared photographs?

10. What is the purpose of a "matching photograph"?

ADDITIONAL RESOURCES

Champod, Christophe; Lennard, Chris J,; Margot, Pierre; Stoilovic, Milutin; (2004) *Fingerprints and Other Ridge Skin Impressions*, CRC Press, Boca Raton, Florida 33431

Cloud Dome (diffusion device), Cloud Dome Inc., P.O. Box 9, Lafayette, CO 80026, (800) 609-8999

Duckworth, John E., (1983) *Forensic Photography*, Charles C. Thomas, Springfield, Illinois 62717

Fisher, Barry A. J., (2003) *Techniques of Crime Scene Investigation*, Seventh Edition, CRC Press, Boca Raton, Florida 33431

Gibson, H. L., (1973) *Medical Photography: Clinical -Ultraviolet - Infrared*, Eastman Kodak Company, Rochester, New York 14650

Hilderbrand, Dwane S., (1999) *Footwear, The Missed Evidence: A Field Guide to the Collection and Preservation of Forensic Footwear Impression Evidence*, Staggs Publishing, Wildomar, California 92595

McDonald, James A., (1992) *Close-up and Macro Photography for Evidence Technicians*, Second Edition, Phototext Books, Palatine, Illinois 60067

Miller, Larry S., (1998) *Police Photography*, Fourth Edition, Anderson Publishing Co., Cincinnati, Ohio 45202

Staggs, Steven, (2005) *Crime Scene and Evidence Photographer's Guide*, Second Edition, Staggs Publishing, Wildomar, California 92595